6. 55

D0858256

LEARNING
TO
BE

*The Psychoeducational Management
of Severely Dysfunctional Children*

by Hanna Bauer

SPECIAL CHILD PUBLICATIONS

© 1974 SPECIAL CHILD PUBLICATIONS
A Division of Bernie Straub Publishing Co., Inc.
4535 Union Bay Place N.E.
Seattle, Washington 98105

Standard Book Number: 0-87562-044-2
Library of Congress Catalog Card Number: 73-81604

Printed in the United States of America

To Mrs. Peggy Kendall
whose sensitivity and skill
provided the matrix for
this search

Hanna Bauer

A sense of wonder and inquiry about the conditions for human change, resulting from her work with severely disturbed children in the Davis Public Schools, led to the discovery and elaboration of psychoeducational approaches to severe behavioral and learning childhood dysfunctions.

Hanna Bauer, Coordinator of Psychological and Social Services and Special Education, Davis Public Schools, Davis, California, developed management strategies to deal even with autistic and schizophrenic young children in their home, community, and school.

As a clinical and educational psychologist (M.A., University of California, Berkeley, Ed.D., University of the Pacific, Stockton), Dr. Bauer holds a clinical appointment in Applied Behavioral Science, child development, and is engaged in the professional training of psychologists, social workers, and educational therapists as well as in program and mental health consultation to schools, clinics, and treatment facilities.

Contents

52889

Preface

The time is now: time to join dialogue, to join action, to share findings, and to combine forces for the provision of services for severely dysfunctional children.

Needed are: research and development, a diversity in provision of care, and the formulation of approaches that lend themselves to rigorous evaluative research. Yet, at this very same time, we must utilize those presently available approaches, limited though they may be, ambiguous though they are, whenever they promise some presently feasible interventions.

This book is addressed to everyone concerned with the welfare of severely dysfunctional children and is presented at this time to provoke discussion, open dialogues, and to stimulate a wide exchange of experiences with any and all habilitative and rehabilitative strategies that have been found viable and which hopefully also will be replicable.

One such approach which seems to have achieved some success is cited here in the wish that such sharing might stimulate others to share their experiences. Many encounters of professionals in the field are needed so that, one day, a cohesive and fully testable theory and practice may be developed. Until then, it is hoped that this presentation will help point us toward this goal.

This book is dedicated to my fellow-workers, educational therapists, paraprofessionals, and aides of the Davis, California, school system, whose skills and personal sensitivities provided the healing power that initiated changes and who developed the basic strategies that lead to a *Learning To Be.*

I thank them for letting me observe, question, and engage in dialogue with them so that together we could discern some of the mainsprings of their craft. I want to give special acknowledgment to those of my fellow administrators who gave permission to innovate and discover, in order to serve children with profound needs.

Yet, this dedication would be incomplete without giving thanks to the patient tolerance and support of my activities by my husband, Herbert Bauer, and the dialogue and the encouragement from my friend and consultant, Edward Rudin, and to the teachers of my early student days: Karl Buehler, J. C. Flugel, E. C. Tolman, and Erik Erikson.

Introduction

This public-school-based model of intervention strategies for severely dysfunctional children provides a working framework for their habilitation. This framework is designed for the use of all personnel concerned or charged with the care of dysfunctional children: the political planner, the administrator of program, the deliverers of primary care, such as health and education staffs, and the providers of direct nurture such as child-care workers and parents.

This presentation is primarily intended to serve as a theoretical framework. The conceptual structure, a bare scaffolding, is discussed in the first two chapters, "The Framework" and "System Properties." Chapters 3 and 4, "Program Components" and "The Special Contributions of Educational Therapy as Therapy," describe examples of practices that have been found helpful. The annotated bibliography cites sources that have been useful as guides to practice.

Each system, each community, must evolve its own practices, based on its particular characteristics, such as the sociocultural givens, the caseload involved, existing administrative structure, and especially the care-giving personnel available. This framework can then serve to organize these characteristics into a specific management system appropriate to a particular time and place. Indeed, not only the care-recipients but also the care-givers and the care-giving systems differ, and, therefore, all these components must be individually assessed before they can be utilized in their own unique manner; only then can their special being provide the matrix for a "learning to be."

As a framework, this presentation provides spaces to insert ideas based on both the presumptive and proven findings regarding management strategies. As a framework, it enables the user to brief out, try out, and confirm or disprove certain parts of his experience, while still retaining a structurally coherent whole and thereby safeguarding the ongoing continued development of a viable structure.

Pending its completion, such a framework is the scaffolding supporting a building until the essential permanent structural members can take over all support functions. As each permanent member is proven and assigned a place to stay, a portion of the temporary framework can be discarded—so that at the end a self-supporting, cohesive structure will emerge. Until such time, in the absence of final tenets, this scaffolding is needed so that necessary action can continue to take place, and work, though temporary and temporizing, may proceed to alleviate the present and pressing human needs of dysfunctional children.

This "action for mental health for children," which is needed now, not only provides the requisite habilitative services for dysfunctional children but also, through change in the change system, creates some important positive social transformations.

While *re*habilitation of the dysfunctional is the ideal target, *habilitation*, enabling them and their environment to learn to make it despite dysfunction, is a realistic and attainable goal. Reaching a level of "social recovery" or greater coping "attainment" with a child who has never adapted in a more functional manner is a tangible and important goal; in the absence of change, the severely dysfunctional must continue to live in an unsocialized, desperately private world, devoid of relational ties, human interactions, or positive self-validation.

At the same time, as habilitation proceeds, the wider society, the change system, and the public school as well gain in this process of care-giving, for through their concern with the humanization of these children they become more humanized also. By dealing with and joining the network of care, the system becomes more caring and giving not only to these special children but to all members of the system. As provisions of support for personnel dealing with the dysfunctional are made, support systems for all personnel receive implicit consideration; as accommodations in the system-structure for special needs for these children are made, other system accommodations become conceivable and often also operational.

The concern of staffs with minimal change and progress in a few very "different" pupils stimulates watchful concern, encourages observation of the many, and an emotional climate where positive change—*minute positive change*—becomes noticed and used for the enhancement of many.

Chapter 1
THE FRAMEWORK

It is also my conviction that, as professionals, we usually do not talk loudly enough to others until we talk plainly to ourselves first.

—Fritz Redl, *When You Deal with Children*

"Learning to be" is a framework for the management of severely dysfunctional children:

Why?

Because of their pressing need for care even in the absence of a proven theoretical or pragmatic management system.

Who?

The severely dysfunctional children, about one in every five hundred, who cannot develop social and educational functions within the context of the usual available growth opportunities. These children, for a variety of causes, are deficient in their basic perceptual, motor, and ego functions and are unable to process and utilize information adequately.

How?

Through the utilization of the public school, a universally available, child-focused institution providing existing physical space, and child-serving personnel.

This management system is based on a model which sees the dysfunctional child in need of biomedical, sociocultural, and psychoeducational supports, in a community which as a network of care is potentiated by a child advocate.

This child advocate assures the optimal use, availability, and continuity of needed care. Advocacy is charged with the task of need assessment, resource procurement, and evaluation, through the provision of management and support skills, thus assuring the appropriate and well-timed delivery of direct and indirect services to procure biomedical, sociocultural, and psychoeducational supplies.

*This framework is based on a model of the organism as a commu-
nicator who is unable not to interact with the environment and who
cannot not change in this process. The environment, at the same
time is seen as incapable of not changing in response to the organism's impact.*

The unmet and poorly met needs of a child population constitute
the *why* of the matter. Some of these children are being erroneously
classified as retarded and are put into programs that are much too
understimulating for their potential growth, some are living at home,
homebound, preparing for total chronic disability, some are institu-
tionalized, trained there to become chronically disabled persons,
some are taken care of in highly expensive treatment centers if their
families are affluent or their community can and will provide such
funds. These many *why's* suggest that we must find a financially
feasible way to effect habilitation; a way that enables the disordered
child to remain within his home community and in which personnel
can be provided in sufficient numbers and with adequate expertise.

The children referred to as being severely dysfunctional are those
children whose functioning is very uneven, who show adequate
coping potentials in some areas, severe deficits in others, whose mode
of relating to other human beings is very limited, and including
some who seemingly fail to recognize their existence. Among them,
some children appear very bizarre, some show repetitive motor behaviors such as rocking and twirling, some appear charmingly non-
involved though less self-absorbed, many lack language entirely, or
only possess echolalic or very limited verbal communication skills.
Many of them develop severe tempers, resist change, and occupy
themselves with perseverative actions. They are prone to panic at
times and appear unfeeling or unresponsive at others.

These are the children for whom this framework attempts to offer a measure of help.

The *who* is this target population: "dysfunctional" children. This strictly descriptive term was chosen to provide a designation devoid of taxonomic or etiological implications in the belief that we are as yet too far from any clear and definitive understanding and do not possess an unequivocal terminology for this very reason.

Thus the term "dysfunctional" is used here to provide a pragmatic nomenclature. We will not disguise our ignorance regarding the nature of the disease processes which produce ego dysfunction in children, but will use the neutral term "dysfunctional" to indicate the behavioral status of such children in need of our care. We are unwilling to get involved here in taxonomic or etiological disagreements regarding the causes of these conditions, and for this particular purpose, in order to get on with the job, will only focus on viable strategies for the alleviation of the problems as presented.

It seems most likely that the symptoms of autism, childhood schizophrenia, and certain severe conduct disorders may represent a large array of differing dysfunctions, all manifesting themselves in the rather limited number of dysfunctional behaviors that human beings can exhibit, such as withdrawal, aggressiveness, learning deficits, bizarre behaviors, and distortions of language function. Like the single cell which has only a limited repertoire of behavior, the organism, too, has only a small number of adaptive behaviors with which to respond to different noxious influences. Thus the behavioral, emotional, or learning aberrations we deal with might also be due to the limited repertoire of possible behaviors in response to different noxious stimuli or deprivations, such as organic damage, developmental lags, or responses to ambiguous communication or malignant social systems, genetic defects, or metabolic disease, each factor alone or in combination. It certainly would be possible that any one of these or a combination of them may be at the root of the behavioral abnormalities we see as dysfunction. Here and now, however, discussion of the causes of such disturbances is temporarily suspended as we must address ourselves solely to the management, habilitation, and alleviation of ego-dysfunctional behaviors.

When specific causes and their specific remediation are found, the work of the "all-purpose alleviator" can become more purposeful and effective. Hopefully this day will come soon. Until such time we must proceed with pragmatic intuition.

The *how* is concerned with the properties of the system, the necessary availability of an advocate, and the contributions of the three support systems to the delivery of care supplies.

The biomedical, sociocultural, and psychoeducational aspects of these strategies will be discussed. However, the psychoeducational component will be presented in greater detail to share some new conceptualizations. This discussion of psychoeducational management involves an attempt to present these approaches in terms of their rationale as specific interventions. In this sense we are not attempting to *find* the prescriptions, but rather to describe their inferred active ingredients or their specific modes of action and thereby discover the nature of such an active ingredient. It is also hoped that this will facilitate replication and a wider use of these psychoeducational strategies if they do prove effective.

Basic Theoretical Assumptions

The concepts on which this framework rests must be stated so as to provide cogency and comprehensibility. With the present state of the art of behavioral sciences, different basic assumptions are possible and each set of assumptions will provide divergent sets of consequents and thus will generate different sets of interventions.

The human model here is seen as an individual in an interactional field, where each *must* communicate with his environment since the individual and his environment constitute an open feedback-loop system in a state of constant flux. Each change in the system invokes other changes, thus interventions—or changes—at any system station will elicit accommodations elsewhere in that system. Thus, interventions may be applied at many different points of leverage: to the care-recipient, or care-givers, to the process of giving care, or to their common environment, or perhaps only to the care-giver's environment—far removed from the care-recipient—in short, at any point of this system that promises changes that might be care-enhancing. In this sense, the *total* environment constitutes this field that can be called a "network of care."

The basic assumption about the nature of the human organism in this system might be depicted by the growing individual as he is moved through his life cycle. This life cycle propels him through sequential genetic stages of physical and psychic developments which in themselves pose developmental tasks, which in turn affect the performance of the tasks of living. The task of individuation, which is basic to the development of a functioning self, is accomplished through the interchange of communications with the total environment, so that the manner in which information is received, processed, stored, and transmitted will determine the functional nature of this organism.

Positive change or learning is facilitated by models who provide life-task-syntonic examples of behaving. Therefore, the behavior processes of the care-givers must reflect or be syntonic with the intended behavior-goal processes of the care-recipient.

Each individual must accommodate himself to his specific developmental equipment, environmental condition, and evolve survival and growth strategies compatible with his status and needs at a given time; thus at times he may be open to inputs, open to rapid change, a state that we presently call "risk-taking"; at other times, he may have to be closed, armored, self-defending, perhaps regressing or standing still, within a network of defenses.

In this model the organism is assumed to have its reasons, operating in a motivational manner as the why and how of the organism protect its inner integrity. These reasons must, therefore, be treated with due respect. This respect is not shown by attacking defenses broadside, and not by imposing external constraints on behavior systems, but by sending messages *permitting* change over long periods of time and in a manner which allows options to the recipient. Such messages, if they allow modifications, can then be picked up by the care-recipient and used to change behavior in an autonomous manner, changing the system into one with different motivational properties that safeguard the organism's integrity, yet allow learning.

The basic needs for each individual in such a system is a feeling of *trust* in the availability of life-preserving supplies. These supplies involve all aspects of necessary nurture, closeness, warmth, and food whenever needed, in both a real and a symbolic manner; in addition, the individual must be able to explore the environment, to change it through his own actions to a point where some closure or completion can be experienced, and develop a sense of personal identity based on a sense of self and a sense of the other. All these are essential antecedents of the capacity to cope with one's environment.

Therefore, all management strategies employed rest on these basic assumptions; the dysfunctional child—the care-recipient—is seen as an experiencing organism, with change potential based on a develop-

19

ing sense of self, as one who is learning to trust, explore, and act. He exists in a human environment, a network of care, composed of caretakers who also are part of this fabric and who, in order to render effective care, also must be able to trust, explore, and act, and possess a clear sense of self.

The title, *Learning To Be,* refers to the fact that the dysfunctional child appears to be deficient in his "being" like a rudderless ship, an intermittently deaf, mute, and blind individual drifting in a timeless and spatially unorganized state. The approach to habilitation of these children involves the acquisition of certain coping behaviors through specific learning processes.

The direction toward normalcy in which these children seem to proceed as they get better appears to be the way in which their basic being becomes more organized in a continuum of time and space with a more clearly identifiable self that they and others can refer to. Therefore, "learning to be" is the direction in which the management of those children needs to proceed. In the following pages we will discuss some of the methods used to gain this end both in terms of administrative provisions as well as in certain specific case management strategies.

Three support systems providing psychoeducational, biomedical, and sociocultural supplies, respectively, are indispensable to the management of severely dysfunctional children. Personnel with expertise in each of these areas must be consulted or actively utilized. A large part of these services are rendered through *indirect* services, with direct services occupying a smaller sector. Much of the specialized service in this model is furnished through *consultation* or on a standby availability basis; direct services involving the need for the continuous presence of highly specialized, scarce personnel requires a cost of time and money which would be prohibitive even if necessary, but certainly prohibitive if not.

The *psychoeducational* support system involves ongoing direct services for learning to be facilitated. The specialized psychoeducational approaches for these children in terms of direct services are discussed in Chapter 4, "The Special Contributions of Educational Therapy."

The *biomedical* support system is part of the professional repertoire of the physician, the physical and occupational therapist, the neurologist, the pediatrician, the psychiatrist, the nurse, the dietician, as well as any other health professional whose knowledge and expertise shed light on the physical needs of a given dysfunctional child.

The *sociocultural* system comprises all of the existing community services in the widest sense of the word, ranging from the nuclear family of the child to the wider community. Service delivery concerns the development and accessibility of the services at the time that they are needed as well as their continued availability as long as they are needed.

The three support systems are facilitated and potentiated by an *advocate*—an administrative coordinator—who must ensure the availability and utilization of services appropriate to the total needs of the dysfunctional child.

With some preservice and inservice, education, and support, personnel already trained in the field of psychology, social work, or special education administration, or with other appropriate experience, could be prepared to serve as administrative coordinators or advocates. The provision, however, of such advocates is essential to ensure the appropriate ongoing, long-term care necessary for the habilitation of severely dysfunctional children.

Chapter 2
SYSTEM PROPERTIES

. . . if we were to take as our concern not the instruction of our children, but the lives of our children, we would find that our schools could be used in a fully regenerative way. . . . We might cease thinking of school as a place, and learn to believe that it is basically relationships: between children and adults, adults and adults, children and other children.

— George Dennison, *The Lives of Children*

The system properties, the system being the *mis en scene* in which the participants perform their tasks, are the primary environmental givens.

The parts of this system indispensable to the habilitation of dysfunctional children are the community as a network of care and the biomedical, sociocultural, and psychoeducational support systems to deliver supplies potentiated by an advocate or case administrator.

THE COMMUNITY AS A NETWORK OF CARE

The *community*, in the ideal sense, is a *network of care and support.* The traditional, tribal, small community represented such a network. It tended to provide care not for all, perhaps, but for most of its members, for it contained a great variety of human models and resources. These derived from direct care relationships based on familial and social obligations and made available a great many different interpersonal relationships. Such relationships serve as supports or role models, and give feedback and confirmation of the self and its behaviors. In such a community, all members have a variety of resources, while at the same time the more troubled, the more difficult, the more dysfunctional still will not become the extreme excruciating burden which their presence would create in the very much smaller and more limited community such as the nuclear family. Thus, members of a nuclear family—a small community of only the parents and siblings, isolated in one small apartment among strangers—become the recipients of all of each others' stressful behaviors. Even when such a unit does not contain a dysfunctional member, such a constant high degree of impact leads to much anger and explosive interpersonal solutions.

In a community that provides many different kinds of people standing in a variety of relationships to each other, such resources dilute and attenuate contacts while at the same time providing supports through the variety of personalities and roles experienced by each member. There can be no doubt that some of the detrimental and agonizing impacts of dealing with people, and particularly dysfunctional people, is due to our present social organization, with its small number of available others and the restricted number of roles and mutual obligations that are available.

In such a limiting society, where a natural network of care and interrelationship is no longer functioning, we must create such a network to habilitate the dysfunctional. Parenthetically, it may be necessary to rethink our entire societal structure, as some of the members of alternative lifestyles have told and shown us, to make life viable and more productive for all of us; however, the dysfunctional certainly have first call on such a restructuring. The care delivery model that is discussed here is one such way of structuring the available life space and is done with comparatively small and inexpensive modifications to meet some of the unmet needs of the dysfunctional child.

The building of a network of care, however, does not imply the creation of new resources but their redeployment to ensure that all available resources are fully utilized as needed. Thus, the provision of a network of care may often only entail supports of presently available caretaking personnel to ensure and enhance their continuing support to the dysfunctional child. Very often the major need here is to provide the kind of support that will enable people to continue to work without seeing change, sometimes even in the face of regression, and still be able to give out those supplies that are needed by the dysfunctional child to maintain himself and to improve his ultimate functioning.

The concept of providing and strengthening a network of care in the child's life space, instead of the creation of new facilities away from his community, allows the child to remain in his home community so that he may learn to cope there. Improvement, if gained away from the home community, usually makes re-entry difficult if not impossible, and, more often than not, leads to a loss of whatever gains had been made outside the home community upon re-entry. On the other hand, gains achieved within and *with* the community tend to remain stable and in our experience often generate further spontaneous improvement.

It might even be stated that as a network of care grows, the fabric of that community also shows spontaneous generation of other assets, becoming a more caring and thereby socially better functioning community. Certainly, where children with severe dysfunction were integrated with "normal children," the normal children have benefited considerably by their contact with the exceptional child. A quality of greater understanding, compassion, and tolerance of differences develops in the normal person over a period of time as he is helped to deal openly with his feelings about differentness within such a network of care. He is thus confirmed as an individual whose feelings are valid and merit respect and consideration by a social fabric that is helpful to each individual member.

CARE-GIVERS

To understand the process of care-giving in such a network of care, the characteristics of helping people must be studied so that their helpfulness can be better utilized.

What are some of the motivations that direct some people into the role of care-givers and helpers? The major roots for such a quest lie either in feelings of having been helpful or needful of help one-self, possible feelings of guilt about not having helped when it has been in our power to be helpful, or sometimes perhaps even of having been harmful instead of helpful to certain significant others. The urge to be helpful, deep within ourselves, usually derives from some feelings of conflict about helpfulness or feelings of discomfort or guilt. Such knowledge in no way denigrates or reduces the act and action of helpfulness but can add to our understanding and thereby assist us in making this helpfulness available in a more continuing and enhancing way.

Because those of us who choose to be helpers are particularly close to feelings of guilt and self-criticism, of feelings of not having succeeded in "doing good," these feelings must be taken into consideration so that they will not inhibit the process of helping.

Guilt has built some beautiful cathedrals in a need to expiate and undo one's sins; as the rock from which cathedrals are built does not seem to suffer from the feeling of having to return favors, the relationship between the donor and the inanimate giver is very simple. However, when *people* are built or people are helped, the residue of guilt in the helper may get in the way in a process that seriously interferes with the act of helping and may create pain in the helped and the helper to their mutual detriment.

The interference created by guilt is one in which the helper, often without consciously wanting or intending to, relates to the person he helps in such a way that he becomes beholden to the helper by "improvement" as payment for having been helped or cared for.

Thus, a need to get results, to respond by "getting better," by "learning," by "behaving better," by "having more fun," by "being less sad," would all be ways in which the return for helping services rendered would have to be paid for. However, if the person being helped, or the dysfunctional child in our model, is to gain from the helping encounter, his improving needs to be in terms of *his* own choice rather than as a reward for the helper.

Therefore, in assisting the caretaker in providing optimal support to the child, we have to ensure that the caretaker will not *need* or request a "reward" from the child, but will be rewarded in other ways, such as through satisfying personal relations and outside activities. The supervisory staff, consultants, and peers are necessary in a continuous reservoir of providing such supplies to the helper. At the same time, a constant well-functioning inner need structure to decrease the interference by guilt and needfulness in the caretaker is important.

The caretaker's ability to allow the child to grow at his own rate, or even regress, must be communicated by the caretaker to his charge. If the caretaker is reasonably free of guilt and aware of his rewards and motivations, he does not have to demand improvement from the child and can be patient, waiting, and truly let the dysfunctional child change at his own autonomous rate. If we provide an administrative climate where there is time, where the demands on the caretakers are not of such a nature that he in turn has to make strong demands on those he is taking care of, this kind of patient waiting and allowing the child his own growth rate will be possible. In this sense, too, as we pointed out elsewhere, the model of an administrative climate that is supportive and patient provides a continuously nourishing climate of staff appreciation which is necessary to make progress possible.

The insidious development of hopelessness and helplessness in the caretakers of severely dysfunctional people also seriously interferes with work performance. The lack of quick success, the slowness of change, and the continuous close interaction with very unhappy, intense, voraciously needful, and sometimes very irritating people, demands constant support services for all such care-giving personnel. Such support is required to counteract the development of highly unhelpful and often negative emotions and feelings which would become mobilized in the caretaker in the absence of succor.

Enabling the caretaker to accept and handle his conflicting feelings about his charges is a prerequisite to the continuous, successful management of the severely dysfunctional.

THE PUBLIC SCHOOL AS A CARE SYSTEM

The most salient points favoring the public school as the basic support system for the habilitation of the severely dysfunctional child is its ubiquitousness, its availability, and the fact that it is staffed by child-oriented personnel.

Also, as normal models are required to normalize learning, the school presents two irrefutable assets: first, that the school *is* the normal workday place assignment for each child, and second, that this school contains the sum total of potentially normal, age-appropriate models of children and adults.

As part of the outside world, the school is a reflection of the rules, powers, and behavior modes of the society it serves. Thus, the school system not only provides a normal life career, but can also be geared to provide the totality of normal experiences in such a way that the dysfunctional child receives only part of the impact. Only as much as the dysfunctional child can handle is "let in," to guard against overloads of experience and resulting defense against all experiencing and interacting. The therapeutic use of the normal environment by the care subsystem for the dysfunctional child dictates that the "real" environment be presented in such an attenuated way that the dysfunctional child can learn to orient himself in this space, with restrictions and selections to be made from the real system, by letting the dysfunctional child be part of a part of this real world of all children.

A "feel" for some of the system properties of the public school system is important in order to be able to utilize its assets and mitigate its liabilities. The prejudices, hierarchical features, structuring repetitions in time and space, the teaching and learning, and the presence and absence of feedback must be acknowledged. The annotated bibliography refers to some specific sources that view the school in terms of communication and systems theory. However, even if we only naively observe the school in terms of system properties, we can still gain information about the specific characteristics that affect specific desired or undesired behaviors, and on the basis of such information system properties can be deployed in the service of care.

THE THREE SUPPORT SYSTEMS

The three support systems which contribute direct and indirect services to the pupil are biomedical, sociocultural, and psychoeducational.

The *biomedical* support system contributes physical diagnosis and knowledge to bring to bear on the physical management both in terms of normal physical care and of therapeutic pharmacological, surgical, and medical supports. Biomedical information contributes data for goal-seeking and management also in the sociocultural and psychoeducational parameters. This support system provides the inputs of occupational and physical therapy, nutrition, maintenance and restoration of health, as well as information about physical aspects of the dysfunctional child's status that may assist in determining the need or absence of need, or usefulness or absence of usefulness, of interventions in the care of the recipient. The fields of medicine: surgery, physical medicine, neurology, endocrinology, occupational therapy, speech pathology, and so forth, are the indispensable support areas that must be consulted, and must be a constant part of the care-giving process.

Much of this biomedical support can be furnished as indirect service in form of ongoing, monitoring consultation to the direct caregivers, with direct interventions to be readily available when such care is needed. The constant watchful awareness of the support team under the focused attention to needs by the advocate assures the provision of needed direct service if and when required.

For purposes of this framework, a statement of the foregoing broad guidelines suffices, since details of the biomedical contributions to the management of dysfunctional children are available in the pediatric literature.

The biomedical support system must be an integral part of the management of dysfunctional children, assuring through team membership and planned periodic review their availability for necessary direct and indirect services. Such availability must be locked into the system at the onset of management by a rigorous *biomedical baseline review* of each case through scheduled periodic ongoing reviews for the duration of care management, including a biomedical discharge summation.

The *sociocultural* support system provides the matrix in which all care-giving takes place, encompassing all societal interpersonal supplies. The specific properties of the sociocultural system of each child will determine the freedoms and constraints of his management. Both the immediate social system, the child's family, neighborhood, extended family and the wider social sphere, the community, the quality of life, the manifest and latent resources constitute this system.

In the section on management strategies, we will discuss some of the ways in which the manifest resources can be adapted, or how latent resources can be potentiated into available ones.

Here, in terms of viewing the sociocultural environment as a system, one must look at the given factors in two ways: first, in terms of what *is* and then in terms of possible freedoms for change or what *could be*. Thus, for instance, when we look at the nuclear family, an assessment of what *is* currently happening must be made; then, and only then, an evaluation of this system in terms of possible and viable interventions becomes feasible. In line with the premise stated previously under basic assumptions, organisms have a reason for behaving the way they do, and viewing a nuclear family as behaving in a seemingly dysfunctional way does not imply that they *can* or *should* behave differently; only if it is found that a different way of behaving might be life-syntonic for them can a move toward such change be effected.

In line with such a systems view, one must also look at the dysfunctional child-member of such a family as being an integral and "fitting" part of his system. Thus, should that dysfunctional child change, his nuclear family system, too, will change, and we must see to it that this happens in a benign direction.

Starting out from the nuclear family, the system resource assessment fans out into the wider societal field, to provide resource data for all stated change needs of the dysfunctional child.

Often, indirect sociocultural supports consist in enabling a fuller use of already available utilization of the wider sociocultural resources to be used by the care-givers. This approach is further discussed in the section on program components. The direct services offered mainly consist of the procurement and utilization of additional or novel community resources for the recipient.

The *psychoeducational* component contributes the greatest direct care sector in this model. The psychoeducational support component is the major direct change strategy involved in the "learning to be," using the slow, direct, feedback-eliciting inputs of educational therapy. The psychoeducational system utilizes the staff teams of educational therapists, psychologists, psychiatrists, language therapists, art therapists, aides, relationship therapists, and others. Separately and in combination they collaborate to provide the matrix within which the dysfunctional child can modify his being in this world. He can learn to modify his data processing, encoding and decoding, his outputs, his overt and covert manner of relating to his environment, and establish those ego functions that will enhance his ability to cope with his environment.

The rationales and strategies of intervention of the psychoeducational approach are elaborated in the chapter on the special contributions of educational therapy.

THE FUNCTION OF AN ADVOCATE

The indispensable pivot of this management system is a person, here called "advocate," who is charged with the assessment of needs and the assessment and procurement of resources, as well as with their continued appropriate utilization. Such an advocate is necessary to assure the ongoing delivery of supplies in the biomedical, sociocultural, and psychoeducational domains; therefore, he must:

(1) Assess the manifest and latent resources;

(2) Procure the necessary resources;

(3) Monitor the needs of caretakers and provide their needed ongoing supports;

(4) Establish and periodically reassess the needs of the care-recipient;

(5) Monitor the changing needs of the recipient in terms of life career tasks and formulate and review appropriate interventions.

The advocate thus is a systems analyst and manager rather than a direct care-giver; his role is to assure that the network of care will give care, will remain able to sustain care, and most of all will provide the appropriate types of care at the appropriate time.

Chapter 3
PROGRAM COMPONENTS

. . . heart and reason can no longer be kept in separate places. Work, and art, family and society can no longer develop in isolation from each other. The daring heart must invade reason with its own living warmth, even if the symmetry of reason must give way to admit love and the pulsation of life.

—Bruno Bettelheim, *The Informed Heart*

Program components specifically concerned with the habilitation of severely dysfunctional children fall into these broad categories:

   (1) *Personnel*

      Parents, educational therapist, paraprofessionals, matrons and aides, principal, child advocate

      Utilization of staff and care personnel

      Professional team

      Preservice and inservice training

   (2) *Administration*

      Staff communication

      Staffing patterns

      Budget and materiel

      Space

      Time

   (3) *Staff support services*

      Consultation and supervision

      Reports and evaluations

   (4) *Resource management*

PERSONNEL

The people in the child's habitat must be considered first. Their action style affects the dysfunctional child's habilitation. The time spent with the child and the quality of the relationship, and the mode of their interaction charts the course of the child's future development. Only clear, unambiguous, congruent, and meaningful messages will effect his ultimate progress. Thus, in terms of personnel provision, the selection, the ongoing training, and the support of care-givers with beneficial characteristics is the major charge to personnel practice and constitutes the fulcrum of habilitation.

While this school-based model makes heavy use of professional personnel presently and potentially available through the school, personnel management also includes paraprofessionals and other community people; most importantly, however, it also deals with the primary community of the dysfunctional child, his parents, relatives, and his neighbors in his "real" world.

Parents

The parents of all children in our culture are charged with the awesome responsibility for the welfare of their children. Being part of our achievement-oriented culture with its strong judgmental reward and punishment system, they are also locked into feelings of profound responsibility for the "outcome" of their ministrations. Often they are made to feel that their children are part of their own being and that their success or lack of success is somehow represented by the level of their children's attainment.

The kind of relationship between parents and children and the various interferences develop because of the success-and-failure orientation concerning the status of the child and the self-image of the parent. Much that is noxious and promoting of stress and emotional and behavioral malfunction stems from this aspect of parent-child relationships. Thus, when a child seems frankly dysfunctional, has difficulties learning and behaving appropriately, and becomes visible in his distress, the parents in our culture usually experience severe feelings of guilt and inadequacy and are thus punished over and beyond their already very painful discomfort of having to deal with, and live with, a highly dysfunctional child.

When parents are plagued by such guilt and discomfort about their child, the child, too, experiences a still greater loss of self-esteem.

He dimly realizes that he somehow contributes to the bad feelings and discomfort of his parents in a way which is beyond his understanding or his control.

The foregoing discussion highlights the impasse at which the parents of dysfunctional children find themselves. Being human, they need defenses to get the necessary comfort for themselves, but as is often the case, these defenses also elicit further complications and worsen the situation through denial, repression, or defensiveness.

It is frequently alleged by parents that they are blamed for the dysfunction in dysfunctional children. One might take exception to the word "blaming" and suggest that parents sometimes "feel" blamed because of the irrational role that our society has handed them and which they have accepted. They feel blame when many of the clinical writers are *not* blaming, but describing a very difficult and extremely painful relationship existing between a dysfunctional child and his parents. Nevertheless, such a description of their relationship is frequently interpreted as being a cause-and-effect connection, although that is not what had been intended.

Be this as it may, it is important that the other, nonparental caregivers of dysfunctional children take a careful and sympathetic look at the parent who is literally "trapped" with a severely dysfunctional person for much of each day and every night for many uninterrupted years. The feeling of hopelessness and helplessness, or of anger that cannot be expressed, of confusion, of being burdened, of being alone, are more than sufficient a burden to make the parents very vulnerable and uncomfortable. What is more, such feelings are less than helpful to the management of difficult individuals.

Therefore, those of us who work as only part-time caretakers and are only charged with the care of these children for a short time each day and for a small portion of the week must acknowledge the difficult and heartbreaking task that these parents perform. Attentive acknowledgment and allowing the very desperate, angry, and helpless feelings of these parents to surface will assist in building a relationship and a bridge of communication with these parents. At the same time, that initial trust can develop which makes collaboration between the parents, the family caretakers, and the community caretakers possible. Parents richly deserve our helping time and all the information that we may have that can be of value and assistance in working through and solving the management problems they continuously face with their children.

The problem of separation is one such an example. The long-term helplessness of these children develops especially close parent-child ties that make their breaking sometimes very difficult. Care personnel must gently assist these parents to help themselves and their children to accomplish such necessary separations. The child, too, often manipulates this situation and uses such reluctance to protect his own anxiety about having to separate. Quite often, the teacher or child-care person who receives a dysfunctional child first thing in the morning and returns him at the end of the day's session can do a great deal to facilitate such leave-taking and separation problems by clarifying the appropriate parental responsibility and by facilitating such action. He can also help by being open about reporting to the parent on the youngster's reactions in his parent's absence. When there are major problems about separation, the child-care workers may bring these into consultation to assess their own feelings about it. Only after having clarified their own feelings about the separation will they be able to do a "clean" job with the children and their parents. If they are currently either very angry with the parent's inability to separate or else overidentify with the parent's pain, they will not be able to assist either parent or child to accomplish this task. However, most of the time these feelings can be resolved in consultation so that the child-care worker can do an adequate job in this initial and important task. The separation experience is the doorway to further "learning to be" and the nature of this transaction will determine the speed and direction of change.

At times a particular child-care worker may not be able to work through this or some other problem in a helpful way but may react to the child and the parent's situation on the basis of his own needs and concerns. Sometimes such needs are so overwhelming for a caretaker that they disqualify him for a particular task. In such a case it is very important that the system acknowledge this realistically without imparting feelings of failure or shame. Such a task must then be turned over to another worker who in this particular case can act more freely and with fewer constraints. Learning to accept that none of us are supermen or superwomen, that we each have our own Achilles heel, different from anybody else's, is a very important learning step for all people-helpers, which will make us more tolerant of the idiosyncrasies of children, parents, and our co-workers. Accepting our own limitations can help us to develop a realistic approach where the best man will do the best job and where the man who cannot do a certain job is no worse for it and will be doing another job well instead.

Attendance in parent groups is not required; different people want counseling at different times and it is unwise to force people into given roles. Furthermore, counseling success with reluctant and unready parents is very limited. Instead, voluntary parent contact, individually and in groups, should be available, as well as regularly scheduled conferences with the parent or parents as a couple, as the case may be. The parents are exposed to at least two different members of the school team in order to increase the probability that they might develop a feeling of closeness and trust to one or the other person. It is most important that there be at least one person on the school staff that each parent can be comfortable with and with whom a trusting relationship is possible. Sometimes the parent is asked to choose after he has met a number of staff members, sometimes we feel our way and try to assign various workers until somebody is found in whom the parent can develop a trust. At times, situations arise where the parents' current awareness and a child's needs conflict. In this case a person other than the "trust" person is called on to provide such services.

Regular child-focused conferences are structured in such a way that the parent is made to feel more comfortable, more secure, less guilty, and can collaborate as a fellow child-care worker with someone on the staff. In dealing with parents, usually the pronoun *we* instead of *you* or *I* is used, indicating that we are fellow-workers in the cause of alleviating the child's suffering.

Periodically, the case administrator will meet with the parents to have firsthand contact and knowledge of the parents, gain sensitivity to their special needs, and to provide resources for them if they are needed. For example, individual counseling resources may be offered; in some cases, placement of a sibling in a cooperative nursery school to help the mother develop social ties with other mothers may be arranged; or facilitation of a parent's attendance at night school may be made to increase the parent's individuation. Occasional exploration of the parents' referral needs to medical or vocational resources are also ways in which the parents are helped into the network of care for the dysfunctional child. Thus, the parent, his feelings, his coping, and his available supplies are a major management resource.

In the ongoing management of the dysfunctional child there are innumerable occasions when active input by the parents is exceedingly valuable. The parents might be assisted to become cognizant of some struggle the child is having and to cope with it in a meaningful way; the parents might be encouraged to share continuously and openly any experiences that they are having with the child at home to shed light on his behavior with the child-care workers.

It is important that parents be considered part of this team, treated as such, with dignity, given to understand that the management system involves many people with differing roles, sometimes shifting roles that constantly need to be reviewed, refined, and redefined for the needs at hand. At the same time, contact with a parent will help to gain for both the parent and child-care workers time perspectives about the change so they can serve and help each other in keeping a measured sense of trust and hope, which is needed by both of them to do the job.

Educational Therapist

The educational therapist's role is discussed in detail in the chapter on the special contributions of educational therapy. At this point we are only concerned with the selection and, later in this section, with the training and support. The educational therapist, in addition to his superior training as a teacher, must also be someone who can face both good and bad feelings in himself and in others, and who can respond to them in an appropriate and congruent way. He must have the ability and willingness *not* to be liked so he can set limits, say "no," and be unpopular if needed. It cannot be stated often enough that such a therapist also must be reasonably free from pervasive ego needs or guilt that would have to be assuaged by the success of his care-recipient. The caretaker must not need tangible success to validate himself. An educational therapist, to be successful with severely dysfunctional youngsters, must have many passions of the heart but few passions of the mind.

Paraprofessionals

The utilization of paraprofessional workers, both paid and volunteer, is probably one of the most important personnel innovations in this field. There are two major reasons for this: one, that there never will be, perhaps there should not be, sufficient professionals to handle the demands for services. More importantly, however, some of the naivete and freshness of the paraprofessionals is an important asset in promoting progress. Sometimes the paraprofessional does not "know" or has not read that the outcome of certain kinds of the disabilities is "hopeless." He does not know that it takes an almost unavailable degree of expertise to deal with certain phenomena and he can therefore step forth like Parsifal, pure in heart and mind, and can capture the Grail—sometimes even oblivious of what he has done. The young and the hopefully naive have a great advantage in dealing with the severely dysfunctional child or adult, and often obtain much better success and greater results than more sophisticated and therefore pessimistic people.

The work of the paraprofessional must be facilitated by continuous monitoring and provision of mental health consultation, as it is important that paraprofessionals as well as all other staff are able to bring to bear the very best they have to offer and can feel free and comfortable enough to use what inner resources need to be used.

In our experience, the provision of a "significant other"—a person who relates exclusively, closely, but without being clinging or demanding, and without "needing" the dysfunctional child— is probably the single most active ingredient in the early habilitation of some of our severely dysfunctional children. The provision of such a person, at the rate of five days a week, one hour a day if at all possible, seems to be of great benefit. We have found that college students who are interested in entering the helping professions and are still at a stage of professional development where their own self-definition and interest in the human condition is very wide, lend themselves very well to this work. They become involved through a contract providing for their growth in the learning about dysfunctional people, learning to "use one's self in a helping way," and by being given the opportunity of relationship through supervision and consultation with a professional person. This makes for a viable and helpful contract, mutually benefitting the dysfunctional child, the student worker, and the management system.

For the long-term, one-to-one relationship person, such as the student paraprofessional, a stated contract between all concerned is essential, including limits on time and responsibility, a definition of the focus of relationship, help with separation, and provision of constant careful supervision. These aspects must be handled appropriately both in the child's best interest as well as for the care-giver's emotional protection and professional growth needs.

Such one-to-one relationships are very deep human encounters in which the well-being of *both* partners must be safeguarded. Risks are always present when one human being becomes very close to another, especially when one of them is a human being entrapped in a painfully complex fate. Each such one-to-one relationship must be carefully planned, beginning with the selection procedure where the care-giver is chosen on basis of his strength and his lack of need for exclusive personal fulfillment from this relationship through a "clean" separation from which both can emerge intact. The two partners must be compatible, possessing some positive attraction to each other; and most important, the contract and continuity of this encounter must be monitored by a skilled and watchfully available supervisor who will not only be ready when called, but whose awareness skills will also often provide signals to arrive on the scene, hopefully even before a crisis is reached.

The even, predictable, and nonmanipulative one-to-one experience of relating, be it over educational, recreational, or "play therapy" activities, appears to be the single most effective approach to the beginning habilitation of dysfunctional children. The "learning to be" seems here to consist in the learning to be human.

Unfortunately, there exists a caste system among the helping professions. This must be curbed so that paraprofessionals with definite care contracts are *treated* as part of the staff, as part of staff meetings, and are included in institutional and system changes if they are to fulfill their helpful function. If they are "used" as some free by-product that fell out of the community, the success with the child will be minimal, their tenure will be transient, and the possibility that by this more harm than good would be done is ever present. However, if treated as a member of the care team, they can fulfill their indispensably valuable role as the significant other.

Matrons and Aides

We have found that full-time matrons or aides to the primary educational therapist are not desirable. If we work with children whose identities are already shifting and tenuous, the establishment of very clear roles of who is who, who is in charge of what, and what is his function, is very important. We found that making the educational therapist the director of the program—*the* one central person who provides the sole continuity—outweighs the advantages of having permanently assigned assistants. Part-time helpers at various times of the day and for various functions are more useful in structuring the identity of all persons involved as well as of the program.

At the same time, it has been found to be most beneficial to present a variety of "others" for the children to rub up against and model from, while preserving the focus of *one* continuing central figure, the educational therapist.

Principal

The primary personnel includes one exceedingly important person in the school system—the principal, who by virtue of being the head of that particular subsystem sets the tone, both in emotional and cognitive terms. If he or she is comfortable, free and easy and open, the system will be that way too. If the principal is uncomfortable, must hide feelings, or feels defensive, it will be impossible to provide the type of open system needed for a functioning special program.

It may be a waste of time and effort to "put" a special program in a school whose head or principal is uncomfortable with that particular mix of children or with a particular program. It is of utmost importance that the program and the children are accepted in the full foreknowledge that they will create administrative headaches and will produce problems that will be both time-consuming and anxiety-producing for the staffs concerned. Thus, only if a principal feels free and comfortable and welcoming about attracting a certain program will it be possible to prepare for and work through those problems that eventually have to be faced. If he feels martyred or forced into such a program, if there is an inability to give of time and of himself, it will be impossible to create clear roles of responsibility and thus evolve a beneficial program. His acceptance and understanding help a program to flourish.

Child Advocate

In most management systems for exceptional children the psychologist is specifically named as the specialist in this role. It may be doubted that the "generic label" of psychologist really encompasses the needed expertise in this field and it could well be that often a professional, bearing a different label, might fill such a role as well or better. Therefore, in briefly describing the roles of the advocate the necessary functions to be performed are cited first, leaving the option open of who could contribute them. Thus, the usual role definition must be examined.

The tasks that must be performed for the management of dysfunctional children are behavioral diagnoses, including an assessment of learning style, socioemotional status, available language and information-processing skills, and an analysis of the style of relating. The focus of diagnosis must not be on the refinement of "what is" or on the labeling aspects, but rather the "what must be" or the "need assessment." Thus, the diagnostic focus here must be on process rather than on status. In this focus, an awareness of the support systems in their present and potential scope must pervade the diagnostic evaluation, so that the outcome of such diagnostic labors will be the deployment or redeployment of resources. In this framework, a knowledge of the potential both of the system and of specific caretakers and strategies is needed, and to unlock them is as important as the knowledge of many tests or remedial devices, drugs, or facilities.

Such a generalist would soon imagine he was walking on, rather than treading water, unless he could maintain a reality focus; he must be a very open and searching individual who will seek and utilize expertise and support freely in the knowledge of his own limitations. He must be a basically hopeful person who can believe in almost unlimited change in the human condition, yet be able to acquiesce in the absence of change.

Thus, the psychologist in this framework is both a systems specialist and an individual-focused clinician, a learning consultant, and a group facilitator. In short, an applied anthropologist, resident in and impinging on the network of care whose center is the dysfunctional child.

The Professional Team

The need for and use of a great variety of professionals in such a variegated support system makes interdisciplinary skills highly prized. The problems and pitfalls that can arise here point up the dangerous deficiencies and errors in the professional training and resulting self-definition of experts. The problems are based on myths that one's special field carries information and solutions unique from and untouched by the lore of other professions. This causes not only personal divisiveness but also the greatest possible interference with concerted problem-solving and progress in expertise.

The thrust of all science to strive toward parsimonious and unitary answers is directly in opposition to the overspecialization and turf-dividing maneuvers of the lower echelon scientist who also happens to perform the role of basic trainer of such professional personnel; thus, many professionals approach team assignments very ill-prepared.

To counteract this, a great deal of time and effort must be spent to help team members to explore roles, vent their feelings, and feel valued and nonthreatened as persons before the work of the day becomes possible. The suction to "get on with the job" without facilitating teamwork first will only lead to management tasks undone while ego trips are embarked upon.

Yet, if such interpersonal and interprofessional issues are mastered, the resulting ability to utilize different expertise makes such an investment of time and effort worthwhile. Often, the helpful efforts that become available may not be the ones which the professional label of that contributor leads us to expect. Thus, physicians may come up with brilliant educational proposals, child-care workers with observations on physical malfunction, social workers with psychodiagnostic data. In such an "open" team, each team member can bring his own contribution which is validated by the team members and utilized on its merits.

The professional team comprises a wide range of skills and experiences and must be deployed on basis of individual attributes rather than by conventional role designation or label. Thus, as in the case of the primary caretaker, who may be any one of a number of persons on the career ladder with the requisite skills, the team member, and the consultant, too, must be chosen and used on such an individual basis. The skills needed range from those usually expected of medicine, psychology, education, and social work to specialized skills such as craft, music, drama, storytelling, or even yoga-breathing technique. The unlimited variety in which meeting many needs is possible is matched only by the variety in which meeting such needs must be done. The plethora of ways in which one can look diagnostically at behavior is matched by the plethora of ways in which such behavior can be responded to. The richness of team selection and input will reflect the richness of this concept.

Selection, Preservice, and Inservice Training

Personnel for roles involving long-term close contact with dysfunctional children must have an openness of self and willingness to
face the good and the bad, the competent and the incompetent
aspects of the self. Such a person must be willing to enter the very
arduous road of long-term "supervision" in the sense that social
work or psychiatry uses the term—namely, an engagement into the
process of relationship and free-floating observation assisted by an
observer who thereby acts as a teacher to the observing person. As
in all apprentice-teacher engagements, the forces defying change
and the forces of entropy vitiate such a relationship; yet only an
ability to tolerate this will gain the necessary freedom that such
long-term apprenticeship brings. Without this learning process, the
depth of possible skill will be shallow and the repertoire available
to the practitioner small, as his own blind spots will obscure the
farther reaches and the more distant goals.

Most of the time, when recruiting staff, we look at presently employed personnel who show exceptional sensitivity, skill in dealing
with a wide variety of individuals, and who express interest in
working with severely dysfunctional individuals. In the selection
process we attempt to screen out people who appear to need such
an assignment as an all-pervasive fulfillment of their lifestyle, and
to recruit those who want such a task in addition to other life experiences, albeit as a very important one.

Often we do not provide or ask for specialized training prior to
commencement of work with the children, except that we suggest
observations of other programs and provide some of the readings
such as those quoted in the annotated bibliography. At that time,
we also provide very frequent and regular contact with the staff
member, working on and working through their experiences, so

that learning occurs in a preceptorial and tutorial frame, the staff member "growing" and "becoming" as his contacts deepen.

Inservice provides a wide variety of offerings. Much inservice consists of peer-consultation and presentation of experiences by staff members through awareness training, communication exercises, and by sharing and teaching others to become competent in skills which have recently been developed by a staff member. Staff meetings and inservice workshops are also part of this preinservice program as well as a ready reference library.

Formal case staff meetings are not held; rather, individual conferences on case or individual programs are set up with each teacher allowing for greater and more intensive relationships. However, brief administrative staff meetings are held approximately once a month, to allow the exchange of nuts-and-bolts information and to drain off some of the administrative static that may have accumulated.

Meetings away from the work place with topics presented by outsiders, provided they are not lecture but experience or involvement oriented, are helpful. It was also found that training in communication skills for congruence and confirmation has been very helpful to the staff and to parents as well, the latter being invited to participate in such training sessions.

We find this program needs continuous input from other systems regarding their practices. Also, staffing of children by other institutions and observing varying programs of a very different nature, such as day treatment centers, nursery schools, and the like, seem to create the necessary out-of-system inputs to keep fresh data coming in. In the absence of external stimulation with its new ideas and without checking and feedback with other information, a closed system would result which would then keep spinning on its own dime.

The training of other professionals, which is done intermittently by offering training institutes to outside staffs, also is very helpful to the resident staff, alerting it to an examination of its own practices and periodically forcing it to question, screen, and re-evaluate, thus keeping its system open. Again, it must be emphasized that personnel dealing with severely dysfunctional children must have a very "full" personal life away from their particular professional activity. Unless they do so, their being will be consumed by the distress and the needfulness of these children. Both for their own personal and their professional survival, involvement in many different other relationships and activities is important. Thus, personnel in this field must have satisfying interpersonal relationships in terms of sex, friendship, and entertainment, and a life full of activities that are rewarding to them and provide interests and self-validation away from their stressful task.

THE ADMINISTRATIVE MANAGEMENT MODEL

The following aspects concerning administrative practice are of special importance in this management model: communication, staffing, budget and materiel, space, and time.

Staff Communication

As the major model-bearers, the program administrator must continuously offer open dialogue, ask that the staff insist on clarification and congruence, and must allow himself openness in expressing true feelings, concerns, or uncertainties, and invite change mediated by interpersonal contact. In this manner, his behavior models what is to occur at the entire staff/staff, and staff/child levels, providing a visible model to examine what works, what does not work, and how one can make it work. The constant need to re-examine, the constant discovery of ghosts in the machine, are all experiences of the reality of human interaction which need to be open for all to see and deal with.

The administrative climate must reflect what *is*, must leave all the negative aspects (in feelings, in misplanning, constraints from within and without the system) open to view, mirroring what is actually happening at each point of the management system. Thus, all participants can be aware of the true reality of their condition and become both observers and participants of the problem-solving activities throughout that system. As the dysfunctional child must be helped in adopting new problem-solving strategies, the system in which he is to learn this also must be engaged in such reality-focused problem solving.

Such visible, systemwide problem solving eliminates too any pretense of omniscience and omnipotence, and thus reflects the human reality. The dysfunctional children who often are caught in such myths benefit from such an open refutation.

Functional administrative communication practice requires the following:

(1) Frequent time to meet, listen, and respond to all members of the system; this involves both scheduled and even more importantly, on-call time.
(2) Modeling open and undistorted sharing of feelings and insights.
(3) Encouragement of constant interchange of information among all concerned.

(4) Sharing of plans and anticipated changes, with encouragement of open reaction to such information.

(5) Opening of channels for both negative and positive feedback on administrative practice—allowing honest evaluation.

(6) Provision of both formal and informal staff meetings.

(7) Availability of both support and consultation from outside his system to the administrator to obtain feedback and checkback for support, validation, and corrective self-examination.

Staffing Patterns

In this model, staffing patterns should be much more flexible than in most other administrative units. Since specialized needs and skills are uniquely distributed, not arranged according to any table of organization, it is therefore desirable that staff be deployed and redeployed according to needs and special skills rather than on the basis of any fixed personnel classification. Often, when this is tried and meets with success it becomes not only permissible but even a preferred practice. Often the usual hierarchical organization based or ranked on job descriptions is of little use in this system, as even the most junior member of the team may be the best central person for the habilitation of a certain child at a certain time with the rest of the staff giving auxiliary services. Such a delivery pattern can be facilitated through administrative openness, through process instead of formal organization alone.

Here again, if the administrator is perceived as being process oriented, the entire staff can become process oriented. The model of focus, as well as the model of practice, will be transmitted throughout the system. In this orientation, the ultimate care-recipient, too, can shift from needing to creating products (some-thing he is usually unable to do to his satisfaction) and can shift to where the doing and the process of creating become his focus and goal.

Staff work which permits flexible staffing, of course, requires a relationship with the staff where self-evaluation of one's tasks and goals are constantly used in helping to define goals. This focus is necessary to provide a basis for assignment and task definition as well as for ongoing task performance. As the care-giver is by defi-nition a helper in the process of learning to cope, the entire staff structure and thus the administrative input must be one of being a helper in the process of learning to cope with the overall task of each subsystem. Again, the role-function and its appropriate performance serves as the indispensable role-model.

This type of role-modeling is always an important part of success-ful administrative process; however, in *this* field, where the pro-cess of change is based on role-model-learning, the role-modeling by the administrator becomes indispensable as it not only serves the ongoing administrative performance but is actually part and parcel of the desired manifest image.

Budget and Materiel

Budget and materiel are certainly important; however, the pro-cesses by which budget and materiel decisions are made appear as important here as the actual monetary givens. Again the decision-making process, the manner in which the staff system copes with-in the reality of its world, provides as much learning as the prod-uct of final figures.

A sample budget for an operation is included in the appendix. The required hardware for such a program can be minimal, the software can often be begged and borrowed; the staff budgets, however, must allow for the variety of consultant and support services as described in the following section. In this model the availability of supports to the care-givers, thus changing the care-giving system into a model of an available supportive network of care, is the single most important budget priority.

Space

The recent attention to ethological factors and living systems has reactivated the study of and the concern with space. The awareness that space and spaces induce feelings, change actions, and increase or decrease effectiveness has been with us for a long time. However, these influences are studied now in more detail. The discussion of social roles and rules and the ploys of self-presentation and social discourse underline the importance of the locale where such interactions take place.

The provision of, and help with, the appropriate use of space is an important administrative and supervisory function. Fortunately, it was found that small rather than large spaces appear more conducive to the intensive management needs of the severely dysfunctional; the centrifugal, unsocialized factors in these children appear to be better contained in small and intimate spaces, provided there also are subspaces to contain aloneness or one-to-oneness. Supervision must help the caretaker to become aware both of his own spatial needs as well as those of the care-recipient.

At the same time, circulation from space to space and places for aloneness and togetherness must be supplied. The flow-plan of human traffic, where you come in, where you rest, where you promote integration into a larger "normal" group, and where you are protected, can be either very conducive to or interfering with desired outcomes.

Of course, spaces given over to severely dysfunctional children must be fully usable and not be so precious, new, or of such a show-place nature that they cannot be used for hard living and acting. When we have to take care of property we cannot take care of the active needs of these children. Often old, shabby, somewhat warren-like houses can best serve the requirements of such programs. The oldness and shabbiness, too, often makes it permissible for children and caretakers to make their own mark on their spaces, such as by painting them or through amateur carpentry. In habilitating such children, their being able to make their own mark on their surround-ings is often part of their earliest positive coping; thus space repre-sents a major care coordinate.

Time

The administrator, in many ways, must provide for the use of time; this may involve the provision of conference times, supervision, re-porting dates, budget submission, etc.; in this way, he functions as the keeper of the calendar and the clock with all the vicissitudes of intervening in a prime area of the life process. This function can put him in and out of phase with the many biological and social clocks of staff and children. As in any other administrative context, the skill and sensitivity of what "has to be done" and what "can be done" determine administrative action.

However, in this system of providing intensive and close input to the management of severely dysfunctional children, it was found that a specific use of contact time is important: in order to maxi-mize the relationship and the interpersonal impact of psychoeducational management, it was found that *very short* but intensive daily time commitments were necessary. Long stretches of time appear to tax the impact-potential and consequently dilute or even minimize the contact.

It has been difficult at times for parents and management to accept the severe time limitation that has been found necessary. Sometimes no more than *one* hour per day of individual contact, and initially less than that, with a slowly increasing time dose of socialization following, is all that should be offered to these children. The socialization exposure, too, involves the one-to-one person as a guide or bridge into the widening social horizon, the function of that adult is to focus attention on the others and on the child's own feelings in the face of such new exposure. The dysfunctional child is never "let" to be, or "let" to observe; instead, the psychosocial and psychoeducational experience is maximized for him through constant interpersonal input and awareness. Therefore, his activities are restricted to the maximum at which the participants can remain *actively* engaged with him in this process.

The discomforts and interpersonal stress caused by the nature of the child's disability tend to evoke adverse reactions in his caretakers. The care-giver must develop escape techniques to protect his own needs; they can be expressed by either withdrawal or anger and often by a combination of both at different times. Therefore, for the development of the child's positive self-image based on his forming a trusting self-enhancing relationship, his primary contact person must not be overloaded with stressful contact, thereby minimizing the need for such escape maneuvers for each contact day.

It has been found necessary to limit the basic ego-synthetic educational time to as short a time as is needed to achieve a relatively benign ego-enhancing and intensive contact. The amount of such time is increased, slowly, in an attempt to avoid overstress and overreaction. It has been found safer to err in this on the conservative side, as undoing overstress and injury to the child's self-esteem and to the educational therapist's therapeutic optimism is much harder to repair.

Other times may be filled with less structured and impact-giving caretakers or with just being; but the psychoeducational contact must not be as time-filling or time-passing as the rest of the day, lest it, too, lapse into chaotic nonbeing, or nonacting, or nonrelating. The time offered for remediation must not be any longer than the amount of total involvement time that can be tolerated.

STAFF SUPPORT SERVICES

The term "support services" is often misunderstood, for culture-based semantic reasons. Even though the time of pioneering has long since past, the term "support" seems to cast an aspersion of weakness on the supporter. Our achievement-oriented culture derives from the myths of pioneer heritage, whose trappings we still worship with its images of strength and independence and fantasies about powerful others and fears of self-weakness. We tend to exaggerate the true powers of those who lack constraints and the weakness of those who function within limits.

When we talk about support services in the army, we certainly do not imply that we see the army as weak; rather, our stereotype of the military is usually one of swashbuckling strength. Perhaps until we can lay the ghost to rest, that the individual "is" or "should be" stronger than the group, and that relying on others signifies weakness, the term "support" needs to be seen in the way in which it is accepted in the army and in industry, where it means to render or receive such services that will make the accomplishment of a given task both possible and successful. Thus, support services to people who have to give out heavily of their own emotional resources, of their own time, their own comfort, and their own feelings consist of services necessary to replenish their resources and to help them remarshal whatever resources they need to perform their duty.

Because of the interpersonal drainage which sooner or later sends caretaking personnel, including parents, either into withdrawal, emotional coldness, or frank escape, a way has to be found to replenish these resources periodically so that this does not have to happen. Such withdrawal is exprienced as desertion or extreme rejection by the child and is therefore extremely countertherapeutic. At the same time, permission for occasional retrenchment must be given to caretakers—permission in the sense that they can accept the idea that there is nothing shameful, incompetent, or weak about having to withdraw temporarily. The child or children, too, need to know that these *are* such temporary retreats to meet the caretaker's own needs. In our culture, it is neither acceptable or thought polite to inform others of the state of one's own fatigue, or needfulness; therefore, the person needing such relief "appears" to shrink from his counterpart instead, leaving a residue of hurt and pain. Once we can learn to state our needs for retreat or withdrawal openly, they can more readily be accepted by others without their having to feel punished, insecure, or unworthy. Even in special education during the last few years, we have learned to accept and honor the need of some children to withdraw from the group, to be by themselves, to be able to cool off, or have stressless solitude, so they can "find" themselves and their feelings. While we used to "put" children in the corner for punishment, we now can "allow" them to separate from the group and can give them the message that this is their right and privilege. We, the adults in the child's environment, have the same needs and the same rights, and must state these clearly.

The support services needed for the successful and expeditious work performance consist of consultation, supervision, and staff meetings.

Consultation and Supervision

Consultation comprises both case consultation and mental health consultation provided both from within and from outside the system. They can be offered both a scheduled and an on-call basis.

Supervision in the widest sense of the word implies staff management practices that enhance the staff member, helping him to reach his fullest possible functional level through provision of dialogue, thinking through, working through, and a feedback system that encourages self-development and growth. The quality of enhancement that this system attempts to convey to the ultimate care-recipient, the dysfunctional child, must also be the mainspring of supervisory practice, in the model-learning-feedback loop that this care-giving system represents.

Staffings are needed to keep information current, attitudes and goals clarified, and again to model successful joint problem-finding and solving.

We find that both on-call support and regular services are required, involving both in-system and outside-of-the-system supports. If we present child-care personnel with profoundly dysfunctional individuals and expect them to relate to them in a continuing and helpful manner, the least we can do is to offer administrative and mental health supports at any time that they are needed.

The case administrator, or advocate, or a person designated by him, who is capable of giving this type of informed support and can offer consultation conducive to the management of the child-care worker's self and the child's self, should be available twenty-four hours a day, seven days a week. In practice, such support will be rarely requested or required at odd hours; however, knowing it is available will make a great deal of difference. It will enable the worker to drain off feelings that accumulate before they become unmanageable and interfere in the treatment relationship, and it will also give a message that full availability is one of the necessary ingredients of the transaction involved in working with the severely dysfunctional. It also recognizes that the child-care worker's deep involvement and investment in the child is appreciated as a significant and important contribution.

The other part of supportive service consists of scheduled sessions, thus allowing preparation and rehearsal of problems for working through. A different ongoing professional relationship develops from scheduled contacts, which again is a model for the ongoing relationship of the care worker with the child. Consultation from outside the system should also be made available at regularly scheduled times even at a moderate rate of frequency.

Besides these in-house support services and the outside consultation, direct services need to be occasionally available. We find that if the policy is fairly open about such requests and about the filling of such requests, these services will not be abused, for the very fact that they are available if needed makes the child-care staff more comfortable and secure in the performance of their duties. It is duly important that such staffs do not feel that the tasks required of them exceed their available expertise or that they might be left stranded with severely dysfunctional people without having resources to work with them. If they feel well supplied, validated as professionals, and given the necessary supports, they can *give* and thus render successful services to the severely dysfunctional.

Case consultation provides expertise from someone who can provide informational data about situations to assist in the care-givers' problem solving. A behavioral scientist can elucidate the meanings of certain behaviors; a physician can explain the effects of certain medications so that the affected child can be managed with better understanding. Expertise may involve the provision of any number of specialized data, helpful in ongoing management. Such case consultation may be in-house, brief, formal or informal, but it is always based on the presence of a question—the attempt to ascertain information—which then can be used in the management.

Mental health consultation, on the other hand, involves the provision of assistance to the person engaged in direct management to help him to become more able and successful in utilizing his own resources in the management process. In this sense, it represents not only a replenishment of supplies, but also a potentiation of all supplies in the service of service.

Mental health consultation input helps the primary caretaker to handle blocks and impediments to his work performance. The blocks that we are concerned with here are often those that occur due to intra- and interpersonal factors that may come between the child and the care-giver. By having ongoing, face-to-face contact with a trusted, skillful consultant, such blocks can be discovered, often early, and handled before too much interference has taken place—interference which may not only halt progress but could cause a serious setback in the relationship between care-giver and child and impede the child's ongoing progress.

In this sense, the concepts of current consultation, seen as the facilitation of the role of the care-giver or whoever has to replenish the supplies of the dysfunctional child, are most useful. These supplies need not only be recharged because of the draining, incessant demands on affective and cognitive skills of the care-giver, but also because the nature of the dysfunction creates some basic interferences. Without such support, anger and despair may be created in the care-giver, leading to gestures or actual actions of abandonment.

The teacher, the aide, the parent, or the child-care worker, or anyone dealing with severely wounded and manipulative individuals, need the support and reassurance that makes it possible for them to stay with such a very difficult and demanding task. If this is not done, the care-giver will become so exhausted that he must, for his own survival, shut himself off from the demands. Such shutting off is experienced as desertion by the child and in fact, *is* a kind of desertion. It is important that in setting up a care system this concept is fully accepted, not only for the fact that this does occur, but also because it is part of a very reasonable and necessary protective mechanism for the caretaker who could not survive emotionally without the safety valve of being able to turn away when overstressed. However, without external support, this turning off becomes either so frequent or so permanent that the dysfunctional child is in fact again deserted, revalidating all that feels bad or destructive in him and will therefore keep him further locked into his dysfunction.

The mental health consultation model requires that the caretakers are being taken care of and given support as part of the performance of their duties; this support includes maximizing their work performance skills by diminishing the interference. The need for both care-giver and care-recipient centered consultation coexists, and it is wise to assess the specific needs for a given service. These approaches should be considered as services are developed and consultation contracts made.

We might point out here that the support-giving is not only necessary for the job, but also happens to be comparatively inexpensive; in terms of actual dollars even more so, considering the effectiveness of the money spent. In the appendix, a financial accounting for one case, including the cost of consulting services, is given at 1971 cost figures, showing how small such actual cost is.

We found that providing for some consultation from outside the system is highly desirable if not indispensable. Skilled outside consultation is able to pick up particularly on system problems which tend not to be brought out within a system. Protectiveness in the face of possible injury to self-esteem or fear of being evaluated or criticized as well as institutional denial tend to submerge such problems. Outside consultants usually can get in touch with such problems and help cope with the ghost in the machine.

Such outside consultation can be available on call but even a minimal schedule monthly, or bimonthly, with meetings scheduled ahead of time, tends to focus personnel on working at their problems through preparation for such consultation and regular rehearsal of what has been discussed and handled.

In the absence of a consultation budget, arrangements may be made where people trained in mental health consultation in various systems agree to exchange time, once a month or once every other month, with their counterparts, thus serving as consultants to the other system without an exchange of currency. This certainly is a possibility in the absence of other fundings. Provision of consultation, however, is essential to the management of dysfunctional children.

Reports and Evaluations

Reports and evaluation have two major purposes: (1) the enhancement of individual management, and (2) program development.
Both are equally important, but involve different kinds of personnel. Often the process of reporting and evaluating is forgotten in
looking at the expected product. In the framework of care-giving,
the *process* of evaluation must be regarded as highly as the product, as the evaluation process strengthens and deepens the evaluator in his relationship and understanding of his subject. At the
same time, asking of questions—which *is* the process of evaluation—
means the asking of specific *questions within the evaluator* who
then will become personally committed to the possible answers.

For these reasons it is suggested that evaluations and report writ-
ings be, as much as possible, directed to the information needs of
the care-givers and that the obtaining of information for purposes
of reporting and evaluating be couched in such terms that the "need
to know" or "find out" *in* the care-giver is tapped, thus making the
report-maker the major beneficiary.

Where the primary care-giver cannot obtain his own answers, he
should at least have part of the formulation of questions so that
answers obtained will have relevance to his transaction with the
care-recipient. The finding and using of evaluative data is increased
and the sheer weight of data accumulation is decreased. It is appall-
ing how many tons of paper contain information about care-recipients unused because the information was obtained without relating
it to the immediate care-givers. Even the most cogent information
is useless unless it serves management or planning needs.

Thus, in this system, the educational therapist is encouraged to ask
management questions and is helped to make assessments of needs

as he becomes aware of required additional interventions. Rather than build extensive dossiers of "testing" which the primary caretakers receive like a book prize at award time, to be cherished but not to be read, the initial evaluation should contain only the irreducible minimum of data to make placement decisions and to obtain the first answers to management questions. From that point on, further questions are answered by observation, or by informal or standardized instruments; they are raised and answered serially in terms of needs and resources available at that time.

The concept of serial assessment has an additional rationale: it is becoming clearer to more and more people who observe and assess human beings that the context of place and time drastically changes evaluative findings. This context, too, of course, changes with each new intervention as with any new experience of the subject. Thus, the very fact that management interventions have taken place will also change the subsequent assessment findings and lead to new updated management recommendations. Such serial assessment will take such changes into consideration and recommendations will be clearly applicable to a specific point in time in the life career of the subject. By the same token, such time relevance makes recommendations for the present status of the case and applicable to his current life-space, rather than to a hypothetical situation. As this management system attempts to maximize intervention time over assessment time, the law of parsimony must be applied to each assessment decision: "Is this assessment necessary? What types of data can it render and how would such data affect the future management process?" If these questions have clear answers, assessment time is time well spent and in fact becomes management time.

Evaluations are made at least quarterly on each individual and annually on program. Such evaluations involve an assessment of coping skills of the children in terms of their products and conduct.

The entire chain of care-givers participates in these evaluations, which in this sense become an ongoing interpersonal review, and provide the baseline data necessary for planning further interventions.

RESOURCE MANAGEMENT

The assessment and deployment of needed sociocultural resources is, next to educational therapy, an indispensable ingredient for the successful school-based management or severely dysfunctional children. A "feel" for the presence of unmet though meetable needs, the ferreting out of latent resources, and their prompt application for the period of time during which they are needed, are skills and talents needed by the advocate or case administrator. The case administrator must develop an attitude of "constant hovering attention" to sociocultural data to help to alert him and to focus on perceived needs and resources.

Developing such attention is akin to the development of other intervention skills in therapy, for instance, by letting one's mind automatically be alerted to a data search and learn to dredge up information relevant to these alerting signals. It is gratifying how serviceable such a process can become and how surely and rapidly appropriate responsiveness can develop.

Such an assessment of both necessary and enriching sociocultural needs must be made frequently, especially as the nature of severe dysfunction often tends to alienate the child and his family from normally available resources and relationships. While we may think of special community resources as those in addition to the usual social resources, it is important to think of many families harboring a dysfunctional person as being cut off even from many of the usual social supports. Babysitters are scarce or unavailable; activities such as churchgoing are cut down or even eliminated because of the presence of an atypical family member; neighbors may have pulled back or are experienced as having pulled back, so that the family lives in much greater social isolation than they normally would. Such isolation tends to increase the atypicality and poverty of resources for such a family unit.

For this reason, help in overall socialization for *all* family members is often needed through the provision of day care, interest groups, contacts with outside groups such as hobbies, education, or church. The dysfunctional child, too, needs consideration; however, a provision of resources for the other members is of equal and sometimes even greater importance. Again, as in other systems dealing with the child, the strengthening of the care-giving potential of each contact person is a prime prerequisite for beneficial management.

Of course, we will think immediately of the recreational and physical facilities such as Cub Scouts, Girl Scouts, Rainbow Girls, and Little League, but it is important to assess very specifically what the child's needs are at the time, what his stress liabilities are, and his social and physical skills. Very often, social resources are prescribed in a rather automatic manner without regard to the needs of the child or to the specific characteristics of the resource. Many of the facilities, if they are not specifically adapted to the child's needs, tend to be too demanding of skills, and too competitive socially, or too full of judgmental potential. If our goal is habilitation, which involves a building of a sense of mastery and competence, it is important that these experiences be tailormade so that mastery and competence will result. Therefore, it becomes a psychoeducational task to prepare the youngster for his new activities. Often he must first reach a level of skill mastery that will make him immediately acceptable to his new peers; by contrast, a youngster without a severe disability could learn such mastery *in* his new setting and manage the necessary social skills. The dysfunctional child must not be asked to learn and practice more than one skill at a time, and thus must learn such skills *before* entrance into a new experience.

It may help to think of a dysfunctional person as one who is just beginning to learn to drive a car. Each component skill, the rapt attention, the seen and unseen hazards, impinge on the confused consciousness of the learner; as he tries to attend to one stimulus, the real or imagined occurrence of another pulls his attention. The anxiety and tension thus created further reduce the effectiveness of action. The dysfunctional child is thus pulled in many directions, his already poor skills are further reduced, and he will need a back-log of mastery just to let him get by. Even then he requires a back-up of human support to allow him to persist. In a way, we must make sure that each new encounter is not just double-safe, but if at all possible, fail-safe.

In assessing and providing social experiences, one has to keep in mind the amount of anxiety and stress that the dysfunctional child may experience in situations that more functional children can cope with, without any special provisions. One such situation is one's entrance and introducing one's self; it seems important that the dysfunctional child be accompanied and be helped with such introductions, with undressing and dressing, with taking a certain amount of banter, and even a certain amount of "pretend" physical threat, that other children take in their stride. It is important that there are people standing by to help a youngster in this and we very often suggest what we call a "bridge person" to be with the youngster, some adult whom he knows very well, like his special college tutor, to facilitate transition into new activities and social groups.

In evaluating available social resources, their acceptability to the parents is important too, and we need to be sensitive about this as they sometimes might assent and follow our advice because they feel we are experts while they themselves might not really approve of the facility or the activity. Sometimes, there are parents with various moral or religious beliefs to whom certain organizations or practices are anathema. It is important that preferences or feelings like these are honored because the child's comfort to a great extent is based on the parents' comfort both with him and with the situation he finds himself in.

Sometimes we find that programs such as 4H or some long-range projects can offer a supportive, comfortable environment. Sometimes one can find sheltered jobs, for instance, scenery painting, before the stress of performance starts. Helping to develop telephone lists, or providing refreshments where there is a good deal of time, are all ways of introducing dysfunctional people to fail-safe social contexts. Organizations such as churches, big brothers, rock societies, astronomy clubs, or art groups, are resources to be considered. Over the years we have found that if there is a specific need that we can pinpoint, it is often possible to find someone in the community able and interested to meet such a need. It is amazing how many prescriptive sociocultural resources can be mobilized if the prescription is made and clearly stated. The finding and selection of camp experiences of intergrade, interage tutoring and socialization are all important resources. One must not forget that the sociocultural helping network is not only waiting to help, but is also waiting to be helped, and that there are many resources in the community to be derived from the loneliness and alienation of potential helpers. Thus, the drawing in of resources to help children is as important and as appropriate a part of the advocacy program as is the provision of outlets for other community members who will benefit by the care-giving.

A careful study of the individual family and neighborhood subcultures is highly important. Such a study must consider how this particular family unit views and experiences atypicality. To become aware of this we need to understand some of the hopes and expectations of the families of origin, their sociocultural background, their belief and expectation system; one must look at the life-career of the child's present nuclear family where in their life cycle they were when their atypical child became manifest; where they are now, and what is the idiosyncratic meaning of having such a child at this particular moment. How does the neighborhood and social kinship group react to the child's presence and how does this family use these experiences?

At the same time the wider relevant society, its hopes and expectations for *all* children and for *different* children, and its capacities for accommodation or nonaccommodation must be evaluated. As in the case of individual interventions, the need and belief structure of the smaller and wider groups must be ascertained and intervention "handles" found. A contract for care, as in the case of a therapeutic contract, can only be drawn up if the givens of the potential care-givers are known, their change potential assessed, and strategies for possible change defined. As in any therapeutic alliance the only possible lever for change is a motive to change which must be in some way syntonic with the desires and goals of the change.

In assessing sociocultural resources, and resources for the care-takers, the parents and child-care workers must also be remembered as care-recipients. It is important that the parents of these children lead full adult lives that are satisfying and away from these children, to help them deal with their offspring. As with other personnel, it is important that much of these activities are not connected with the child, but consist of broad, fulfilling, social and recreational outlets, in order to help the parents grow independently along with their parenthood role, and the other caregivers from their charges.

Helping dysfunctional people experience their community as being helpful, interesting, and interested is very important. Their sense of alienation, helplessness, and anger can yield much of its sting if they feel supported, wanted, and comfortable within a context of some ongoing social fabric. Learning about the resources and their use is an important part of learning management skills. Learning to live more fully within the social fabric is a learning-to-be.

Chapter 4
CONTRIBUTIONS OF EDUCATIONAL THERAPY

We have learned too that the "arts" of sensing and knowing, consist in honoring our highly limited capacity for taking in and processing information. We honor that capacity by learning the methods of compacting vast ranges of experience in economical symbols—concepts, language, metaphor, myth, formulae; the price of failing at this art is either to be trapped in a confined world of experience or to be the victim of an overload of information.
  —Jerome Bruner, *On Knowing—Essays for the Left Hand*

Anxiety is the dizziness of freedom; he therefore who has learned rightly to be anxious has learned the most important thing.
  —Soren Kierkegaard

The child, on the other hand, will identify not only with the teacher's love of knowledge, or mastery of subject, but his ways of searching, of allowing differences of opinion. . . .
  —Rudolf Ekstein and R. L. Motto, *From Learning for Love to Love of Learning*

The specialized contributions of educational therapy provide the matrix for such information processing and for behavior modification that makes subsequent changes possible. In this section, some of the specific technical contributions of educational therapy will be discussed; in addition, the presumptive active ingredients peculiar to educational therapy will be examined. A clinical description of the activities of successful educational therapists will be described to highlight the healing components of their activities.

THE JOB OF THE EDUCATIONAL THERAPIST
EDUCATIONAL THERAPY VISITED

In the following section a descriptive job analysis of educational therapy is presented. The teaching-learning paradigm of the establishment of better ego functions for the severely dysfunctional is described in the section on ego synthesis. The section on the therapeutic curriculum and curricular therapy examines process and content of the curriculum, tying and untying the interpersonal components.

While the special contributions of educational therapy to the habilitation of these children is invaluable, only the total system can provide the matrix for ongoing successful management. No single component alone can carry the load, while even a moderate though integrated effort of all support systems promises much success.

The heading for this section, "Educational Therapy Visited," was chosen because the material presented here was obtained from observation of educational therapists at their work. As a coordinator of services for special students, the author visited many educational therapists and observed and discussed their teaching plans, techniques, and progress with them individually, in groups, and in seminars. The materials presented here originate from the practice

of educational therapy but are viewed through the eyes of a psychologist, and not the therapists themselves. Yet, over the years,
many hours of dialogue as well as an analysis of therapists' practices have provided these observations. Had an educational therapist reported here, the more conventional title "Techniques of Educational Therapy," might have been legitimately chosen.

These observations were made of individual and small group teaching sessions dealing with severely dysfunctional students ages four
to eleven. Initially, many of these students were verbally incoherent, socially tenuously related, and psychologically often not "testable." Still, each of them showed some splinter skill or aptitude
which made their classification as being only "trainable" inadvis-
able at that time. Some of these students presented a very grim
prognosis and it probably was due to our own blithe ignorance and
inexperience that let us proceed on this educational venture which
resulted in a slow but significant functional improvement in these
students.

These students required interventions in all four goal areas of educational therapy: attention was fleeting at best, input and output
functions were seriously impaired while their cognitive strategies
were haphazardly primitive, and their executive ego functions
chaotic or at times even absent. However, a need to provide basic
teaching services for them forced us to look carefully at what we
appeared to be doing, what appeared to be happening, and especially what appeared to be effective.

As yet, there is no "proof" that our approaches provided the
change agents that triggered this astonishing growth, as the sheer
passage of time may have accounted for change. For some children, improvement was the only way to go. Still, the same methods applied to a number of similarly severely affected students

which resulted in similar significant developmental gains. We hope that this publication will lead to further exploration, replication, and evaluative studies.

We always insist that even severely dysfunctional children leave home for the teaching session, believing that the time-and-place-structuring implicit in this requirement is necessary and that the parent-child separation also constitutes a necessary learning task. Often a senior or graduate student was provided for three to five hours per week to give additional specified educational training, such as language stimulation, motor or movement exploration skills, or sometimes to provide additional opportunity for a clear, ego-enhancing relationship with another concerned, though non-involved, human being.

Educational therapists function in these four domains: (1) information processing; (2) cognitive strategies; (3) input and output skills; (4) executive ego functions.

Information Processing
Obtaining Focal Attention

Obviously, the first task of teaching is to secure "focal attention" and to sustain it for the duration of the teaching session. Teachers have many with techniques for this. The educational therapist has no new magic here, except for an even greater awareness of the discouraging effect that the pupil's real or imagined nonattention can have on the teacher. In fact, often these children later show that they had attended, so that the teacher should assume that he is being heard unless proven otherwise. On the other hand, pushing for confirmation will only raise the teacher's frustration. While the regular classroom teacher may ask for confirmation too often, the educational therapist usually allows the student to confirm or not to confirm receipt of a message as he desires. Then the message becomes one of autonomy, keeping the pupil outside the teacher's need of *having* to be confirmed and reconfirmed.

"Orienting" and "set" are obtained through space or position, time, and verbal cues. The therapist will say: "After recess, I will go with you to your desk and after you sit down I will show you how to trace your name." This type of message invokes the necessary *anticipatory set* and provides preparatory rehearsal.

Experienced therapists seem to use such cues repeatedly during each session; these cues provide the essential coordinates for the pupil, guide and organize his actions, provide a preliminary workset, and tie his activities into a time and space continuum. A previously disorganized student slowly appears to "have it all together," attending and responding each time the therapist comments on this aspect of the performance, making this process the main target. Also, each hit is recorded in terms of its closeness to the mark of the desired behavior.

Pupil attention should be volitional and is only useful if freely given; histrionics, of course, can capture transient attention, but this is not the type of attention that a learning-handicapped student needs to master. Therefore, the teacher eventually must enlist the student's own intent to attend.

The successful educational therapist seems to attain this by using spatial and temporal clues and involving the student both in the planning and evaluating of each activity. A clear statement of "where" and "when" "what" is being done is required. Suggesting to the student to come to such and such a place when he is ready to do a certain task builds up his autonomy of action as well as his attentional control by providing cues to induce set and orienting behavior. This approach does not preclude certain task demands, such as needing to complete a task before a free activity becomes available; still, it must be the pupil who initiates the sequence.

Another reason for eliminating the nagging type of request for attention or confirmation of attention is its destructive impact on both the therapist's and student's self-image. If continued, this action would seem to say to the students: "You make me feel bad; by not being listened to I feel unimportant and a poor teacher; if you make me feel bad, *you* must be bad." Removing the basis for this sequence thus eliminates a major irritant.

As teachers discover that their pupil's inattention is not directed against them, they develop a new awareness of the dysfunctional student's needs for attending to whatever it may be he was attending to and his problem in shifting his attention. The bridge a teacher must cross to change from a *remedial* teacher to an *educational therapist* might well be his awareness that "the mind has its own reasons." Somewhere an awareness of the integrity of the dysfunctional child, and recognition that even the dysfunction is a valid part of this child, probably a necessary part, changes teacher behavior permanently. The result of such awareness is not complete license "not" to engage with or follow the therapist, but rather a stance that invites and permits and facilitates attention to the therapist's messages, with the added result that most of them will eventually be attended to.

The dysfunctional child also hears many outer noises which he can and must sort out and yet progress while hearing many inner voices. These inner voices may be self-stimulations, fantasies, or intended rehearsed responses; no matter what, one must not intrude directly, but continue to provide relevant input. It is often surprising how much has been perceived after all. In a few instances, such confirmation comes in as long as two years after the event.

When left without external stimulation, some autistic-like children become more withdrawn and abstracted, more drawn toward their inner voices. In a few of them, "wiring for input" appeared to help their attention capacity to an amazing degree. For their art work, perceptual, or reading exercises, an earphone feeding music appeared to satisfy a need for sensory stimulation which could otherwise only be filled through direct active relationship with a teacher-involving auditory and tactile contact, or else rhythmic self-stimulation would recur. Paradoxically, then, in some dysfunctional children, adding what would be distraction to the normal child appears to increase and sustain selective attention.

Storage and Retrieval of Information

In describing strategies to promote better "storage and retrieval" capacity of the mind, the analogy of a library or file system might be used. Before places for specific types of books have been designated, they might be piled up helter-skelter—*there* they are, yes, but virtually impossible to find. The storage and retrieval facility of the dysfunctional pupil resembles such a haphazard system. While the functioning pupil, even at early school age, comes equipped with "filing" or shelving skills, the dysfunctional student is usually deficient.

Sometimes we can find out whether this lack is due to language deficits, primary process intrusion, perceptual inconsistencies, or a combination of these. But whatever the etiology, the student must gain good functional efficiency in this area if learning is to progress.

The teaching approach is tediously slow at first, as the educational therapist prepares the "location" for incoming data storage. "This is another zoo animal," says the teacher, as he shows a picture or word denoting a previously unknown animal. Such *advance labeling* becomes second nature to the therapist and serves as a storage location trial. "What new zoo animal did you learn about today?" is a practice in firming up associational links. The teaching that is done here goes far beyond the teaching of the specific item. It represents the building of an effective storage and retrieval system, bringing order to chaos by making information accessible to demand.

The educational therapist strives for better memory consolidation. The time lag normally required to move information from short-term to long-term memory storage is longer in many dysfunctional pupils. Therefore the educational therapist continues to practice recall and reinforcement long past the usual five-minute consolidation time; often for hours, days, and weeks. Each recall trial utilizes the association *filing cues* plus additional associational material learned prior to, or subsequent to, initial exposure to a specific informational bit.

The most successful learning of storage and retrieval techniques occurs when the teacher utilizes material that is relevant to the pupil and which has high affective survival or coping value for him. Sylvia Warner's Organic Vocabulary is such an example. Associational chains, techniques for developing classes of associations, or tying them in a cross-reference manner to other information, develop most rapidly when the student is personally involved in the content to be learned. Still, special attention must be paid to the process of "how to store" and "how to retrieve," regardless of the relevance of the material that is being stored or is being retrieved.

The teacher has his greatest positive impact when he produces learning materials as the student watches. This may be due to the combination of a number of beneficial factors, such as the obvious personal interest expressed for the student and the consequent increased set orientation, and the readiness created within the pupil. Watching the process of making a lesson seems to create greater perceptual impact, like watching a moving versus a stationary stimulus. While watching the unfolding of the task much inner rehearsal and solution finding appears to occur and thereby to increase total practice time. Also, at times, the student may learn what he needs to learn as he thinks with his teacher in evolving this task. Teacher-made materials, and especially *teacher-made-materials in the presence of the pupil,* appear to be many times as valuable as the most brilliant teaching device brought in from outside the therapist-pupil relationship.

At the same time, to be accessible to intervention the output response must occur in front of the teacher's eyes and ears; not only so that the very important immediate feedback-and-correction effect can take place but also so that the relationship aspects may enhance function, and that process rather than product can be monitored. Involving the pupil in originating questions and tasks to aid his performance provides him with an opportunity for both cognitive and motivational participation.

When he has mastered his material, the student acknowledges success with visible pleasure. Whether this is "learned" pleasure based on subtle or strong teacher reward or is based on a feeling of closure or decreased dissonance seems immaterial. The student feels success and uses this success to venture further.

Improving Cognitive Strategies

The development of "cognitive strategies" has one important pre-requisite for the educational therapist: he must be a skilled thinker himself. Unless the therapist is able to execute cognitive maneuvers with sequence, logic, and efficiency he will not be able to act as a model for his pupil.

There are three approaches involved: first, the use of continuous, role-modeling by the teacher who appears thoughtful, taking time to formulate questions, and to find answers which he always tests. Impaired thinkers appear to have much trouble in dealing with the intervening steps in cognition; they need to articulate the middle terms by always stating them explicitly. They must see how one gets from here to there. Much of their mystification about the world around them has not to do with their perception of the origins and the destinations but with their ignorance about the road traveled between these points. Here the teacher must think transparently and publicly, accounting for each step, each process, and for all supporting or corroborating facts that contributed to the solution.

The clarification of the supporting evidence is important. The message: "It is cold, the thermometer is at freezing," is lacking the statement "the line is at $30°$," which is what really provided the evidence. Not redundance, but gap-free sequence is needed. This slowing down in process is difficult at first, tedious and time-consuming, but it is learned more easily as the pupil rewards the therapist with increased cognitive powers.

The second path involves an awareness that dysfunctional students often fail to utilize entire classes of data and thereby may miss their cognitive marks. Sometimes, this may be due to perceptual dysfunctions, at other times to denial or repression. As the therapist becomes alert to such omissions, he learns to fill them in. Some pupils will cut out certain sensory channels; some, for instance, cannot or will not utilize auditory or visual aspects of data; others will distort or deny so that houses may never have doors, or fire seems not to exist, or human faces lack mouths. While a psychotherapist or behavior modifier would work on the content problem, the educational therapist will be concerned with the cognitive gap in a reality-oriented cognitive setting. While this may be a type of "working through," the focus and technique is different; it does not deal with or remove the underlying cause, but instead helps to rehabilitate function. This latter approach to cognition enlarges the cognitive domain of the pupil.

The third approach leads from the more immediate sensorimotor-based experience through operational to transformational and abstract or symbolic levels. While this strategy appears closest to the traditional thinking approach, the educational therapist proceeds more slowly, covers all bases through checkback and feedback, and remains on the lookout for magic or pseudosolutions that are offered by his pupil. Both functioning and nonfunctioning individuals employ logic. The dysfunctional logic, however, is often idiosyncratic, distorted by the differing perceptual and mental processes of the dysfunction. Traveling from primitive to advanced cognition and from personalized to generalized logic points the road toward functional efficiency.

The terms *walk-through* and *rehearsal* spring to mind in describing the manner in which an educational therapist teaches thinking skills. He must walk-through and patiently rehearse, step by step, line by line, until the play is down pat.

Input and Output Skills

The regular classroom is devoted to the development or sometimes just to an exhibition of various "output skills." From coloring within the lines to the writing of term papers, from hopscotch to team football, the normally growing child earns his educational Brownie points or Scout ranks by turning in his output badges. The dysfunctional student is unable to earn these marks of educational worth. His pervasive deficiencies in information gathering and cognitive power alone would preclude his success; however, dysfunctional students may also have deficiencies in expressive language, perceptual or motor efficiency, or have problems of dyspraxia or sequencing. Integration of sensory modalities or difficulty in utilizing cross-modal cues also makes him a poor performer.

The fantasy that even a very good psychologist should be able to "diagnose" or describe the totality of a pupil's functioning during a few brief encounters comes to a particularly sad end in this area. Many rather minute but important deviations come to the fore after months of educational therapy. The educational therapist must become an astute clinical observer on the alert for uneven functions; he provides special practice if that seems feasible, or helps desensitize the pupil realistically if a certain type of skill is unattainable.

Promising the blind that we can teach him to see is as unkind and destructive as any promise of functional ease for an area of profound deficit. Instead, the therapist must look for compensatory skills. Evaluating realistically what is possible, what may become eventually possible, and what seems impossible is an important part of reality testing both for the pupil and the educational therapist.

Perceptual Sorting, Channeling and Language Training

Perceptual sorting, channeling, and language training provide augmented input and output skills. The therapist often acts as a perceptual sorter and has to recreate or restructure the perceptual world for his students. For some a stark simplification of stimuli is necessary, for others a reduction of stimuli to only one sensory modality is needed, while for another group an integration of one or more senses is required.

Like Anne Sullivan, the prototype of the educational therapist working with input-output channels, other therapists too must observe carefully to try to find the best way in which a student can deal with stimulus material. To permit growth as the pupil's capacities change, the input patterns also must change. Readiness for different or additional input can only be ascertained by observation and trial; therefore, this process is one of ongoing experimentation, verification, and modification.

For the majority of pupils, multimodal input appears most effective where gestures are reinforced with words, pictures with sound, sound with kinesthesia, touching, and feeling—some or all are called in to describe the present varied sensorimotor world. Without specific input about the world around him, the pupil is unable to learn to cope with his world—in short, is unable to learn. One of the reasons for the variety of inputs provided is our ignorance about the way in which each of our students really learn.

While this basic sensorimotor input occurs, cognitive encoding accompanies the process. Picture, language, and gesture, representation in clay, crayon, sound, photograph, or word are all symbolic cognitive representational encoding experiences.

The game of concentration appears ubiquitously in academic therapy groups. Its teaching values (though rather deadly as a game) are threefold: it lengthens attention, sharpens perception, and calls upon a "decentration" by requiring that an absent stimulus be memory encoded. This sound teaching substance of a less-than-exciting game can be incorporated in many daily training activities.

Bruner's sequence of *enactive, eidetic,* and *iconic* encoding—the motor act, the picture, and the symbol—is a useful guide to the multiple-encoding strategy for teaching. In order to cover all bases, to open all gates of the mind, or sometimes just to try to chance to find one open, such a multisensory as well as multicognitive approach must be used.

Teaching proceeds by "telling," "showing," or a combination of both, learning through enactive, eidetic, or symbolic encoding of what has been shown or told. The enactive mode requires much direct, active role modeling; thus, the therapist plays out the cues, the pupil mirrors; the iconic mode permits some representational input, the confirmatory feedback consists in either parallel production or even a recall of features of the original image; the symbolic encoding not only permits the use of symbol systems that are not representational of their referent, but also involves inferences or a filling in for incomplete data. By presenting information in such a multiple manner, the student's data-processing range widens.

"Games" of many descriptions lend themselves as vehicles of multi-representation, enlisting a variety of necessary coping skills. Games are not "only" games, they are really games; they serve as the playing fields of Eton to the empire of the mind; their "as ifness" increases their emotional safety; they represent "time out" to threatened self-esteem while at the same time providing a plethora of per-

ceptual, motor, and cognitive as well as social tasks. The therapist's strength lies in his ability to ferret out what types of
skills the pupil requires at this time, but even more important,
what skills are inherent in a given game under a given set of
rules.

"Old Maid" or "Go Fish," for instance, may be used to exercise one or more of the following: attention, the motor skill of
shuffling and dealing, the ordinal skill in dealing correctly, the
recall and practice of rules, sequence of turn-taking, sequence
of stimulus-response-cause-and-effect, perceptual speed and recognition, a combination of motor-perceptual-and-language acts,
initiation and stopping an activity in a time and place setting,
the "reading" of the other, giving and receiving interpersonal
feedback, and so on. The massive content of such a seemingly
simple game and its potential for meaningful and sequential educational therapy interventions is stupendous. The art and skill of
need-diagnosis and the application of remedies is well exempli-
fied in the use of games; perhaps instructing educational therapists in the use of such games might be a worthwhile experi-
ment in teaching the technology of educational therapy.

Often a dysfunctional child can perceive and decode only certain
types of material. For example, he may be unable to compre-
hend gestures but be able to decode the words naming such gestures. When such apraxia is complete, of course, words will have
to serve in lieu of gestures; however, if incomplete—and it is
safer to assume that partial function may be available—both gesture and word are presented so that gestural language may slowly
be learned. This approach holds true for all other sensory chan-
nel deficiencies and for all types of communications.

Here, chronological, narrative records of the training transaction are indispensable, as they provide the clues to the specific information-processing style of a student and of successful and unsuccessful teaching strategies. Both the art and the science of educational therapy derive from such ongoing, minute observation and the future interactions derived from them.

Learning proceeds from brief focal attention through selective and then to sustained attention, from "Look, John—a green triangle," to a secure attainment of perceptual targets, and finally to perceptual generalizations based on many successful input experiences aided by competent memory work. Comparisons—at first of simultaneously presented data as they do not use memory or visualization—are followed by sequential comparisons which give the dysfunctional child a stabler perceptual world, with a past, present, and an expected future. The stability of remembered percepts—knowing what something looked like yesterday at dusk, and today at noon—gives stability to the world and makes coping possible.

The teacher may "point" to the stimulus, "walk" the student "to" it, "walk out" the stimulus patterns, or "trace" or "reproduce" it in many media—soft, hard, smooth, or rough; or again the teacher may outline the stimulus by gesture, speak it for auditory input, have the pupil say it for auditory-self-feedback, and he may reinforce it through speech and other skeletal muscles so that proprioceptive or internal stimuli reinforce the external data. Conveying information along many simultaneous and sequential channels is one of the educational therapist's special skills. He performs as a mime, an actor, speaking like a simultaneous translator in many languages. As a matter of fact, mime, acting, and other expressive training is a most useful skill for educational therapists. Also, awareness training provided by certain nonverbal "exercises" are helpful tools for the therapist.

Motor Channeling

While the normally developing child acquires motor skills on his own, the dysfunctional child may have significant motor deficits. As in the sensory area, these may be very spotty, with some skills developmentally normal, some superior, some deficient, and some virtually absent. Splinter skills—isolated nonintegrated motor skills—occasionally mask serious underlying system deficits. Again, careful ongoing observations are necessary to develop a continued good treatment plan.

Some children, as their general coping skills improve, also improve in many of their motor skills without special motor training. These are usually children whose motoric unfolding was stultified by their pervasive anxiety; literally, their fears of living and their poor perceptual and cognitive preparation for it had them bound up. Such children develop functional motor skills rapidly along with other improvement and by the same token are highly resistant to motor training before that time.

In most children, a process of "motor channeling" involves integrating focal and sustained attention, so that motor acts become volitional. Making the motor apparatus more responsive and capable improves the bruised self-image of the dysfunctional student. He must be helped through external cues—voice, sound, visual signals—to start, modify, or stop his motor productions. By becoming aware of his body, which he may have practically disowned, its size, shape and interrelationships, he can obtain better physical command. The educational therapist's accepting attention to his body helps to define it as worthwhile, important, and knowable; seeing, touching, and feeling his body, naming its parts, getting to know function, representing it in picture, photographs, movies, television, by himself, by his teacher or peers, makes it more familiar, acceptable, and ultimately more usable and thus helps to create a "good" self.

Language training (not speech therapy, which has to do only with the sound production aspects of language) is a new but important applied science concerned with the improvement of receptive, inner, and expressive language. We found that careful attention to the pupil's individual expressive language style is very fruitful; we are learning to hear and respond not only to what he says but how he says it, and find that his own language becomes freer and more openly communicative once his own private language has been heard. As painful as repetitious language can be, we have learned that his vacuous-seeming, repetitious language often holds important cues that he wants to transmit. Only when this cue is responded to can he leave this repetitive verbal or nonverbal communication.

The four domains of educational therapy discussed here seem to be in hierarchical order. While without focal attention learning about the external world is impossible, each added skill contributes to the attainment of healthy ego functions: unless information can be taken in and stored where it can be used, unless the child knows and "owns" his body, his self will be tenuous. Unless he can live in a time and a space which he can understand and fit to his needs, he will have to reside in limbo—dependent, confused, and noncoping.

The most important rehabilitative function of the educational therapist is then to combine these first three most basic skills of attending, using cognitive strategies, developing perceptual sorting and motor skills in such a way that the pupil can become an independent, self-differentiated person able to plan, initiate, and execute tasks and evaluate them with appropriate amounts of independence or dependence on other people.

Building to Provide Executive Ego Function

Successful educational therapists use some of the following strategies to enhance their pupils' ego functions as they consistently confirm their own and the pupil's selfhood. "We" never do "our" spelling, "you" do "your" spelling. "We" are never angry, either "you are" or "I am." The teacher signals his and the pupil's separateness at all times. The actor and the acted on are always clearly designated, and in spite of great closeness and concern the symbiotic confusion of identity is avoided. Many of our children, when first seen had great difficulty with their pronouns, their names, and obviously their self-delineation. Thus, "who" does what, "who" wants what, and "who" feels how are very crucial matters.

At the same time, we find that many of these children are exceptionally sensitive to moods around them; anger or sadness needs to be bared to be dealt with, annoyance expressed, disappointment expressed. The predictable congruence of the therapist's communications, words, gestures, and deeds, are an indispensable foundation for the reality-oriented habilitation of the student. Sometimes the therapist's consultant may have to point out inconsistencies; sometimes television taping and replay help ferret out incongruencies. At the same time, the educational therapist is alert to such incongruences in the pupil too, and assists him towards more congruent communication by making openness safe, where feelings can be honestly dealt with by both pupil and teacher.

The limbo of time and space confusion apparently can be dealt with at the level of *task planning, task performance,* and *evaluation.* The coordinates of "first" and "later," "before" and "after," "inside" and "outside," "at the desk," "on the rug," "before or after recess," "yesterday morning," "tomorrow night," "before Christmas," or "after summer vacation," give many temporal-spatial experiences. If a predictable causality of both adult behavior and consequent events accompanies these, the pupil appears not only to "learn" these concepts but, even more important, to "use" them in finding order in his life. Thus, this approach of educational training gives him information as to "who" he is, and "when" and "where" he is living out his existence. We have seen much pleasure radiate from a child's face when he suddenly finds that tomorrow does come with some predictable event, and that yesterday has some shared reality between him and his teacher and his peers. His sense of trust becomes also validated as this shared reality contains both the good and bad of all shared human reality. The events that make life real for real people must be dealt with openly and with their full complement of feelings so that the intact congruence of two human beings can be experienced.

Separation, sickness, and death are some of those reality crises. As a culture, we often tend to deny their reality; the dysfunctional child who is already caught up in a whirl of uncertainties sometimes is seen as one who needs special sheltering. However, we have found that his needs are for more, not less, exposure to reality, for more clarification, more staying with even grief and anguish.

One of our students who has made the most remarkable progress shared with us, as he gained language, how fragmented and confused he had felt about absences and separation. He confused even minor separations with death and appeared to believe that absence somehow dissolved people's bodies into the frightening incoherence that had been his confused body image. The shared reality of learning with his trusted teacher, about bodies, leaving, and temporary absences, provided a wealth of reading words, play, and language sequence, accompanied by a new mastery of living.

94

There is a move abroad to return the regular classroom to life; the educational therapy room always had to be part of living.

In this context, the question of socialization with peers arises. In our programs we have always provided at least some exposure to functioning peers, believing that all learning utilizes role models and that if our goal was eventual integration, "normal" students had to be experienced. At the same time, if we are to be realistic, we had to acknowledge that most of our beginning students were very much out of touch with their peers.

We know and relearned from our students that a firm perception of his self and a basic awareness of this self as an experiencing unit had to precede any true socialization. We also found that a pupil's ability to decentrate and to show a stable self-concept would closely precede his first genuine social relations. This socialization, too, becomes a part of the curriculum, testing perceptions, rehearsing input and output modes of response, and evaluating the new other by the tools of recently learned and practiced self-evaluation. Sorting out what can be observed from what can only be surmised, asking, getting, and using feedback, all these are the basic tools of educational therapy.

Some of the pervasively deficient pupils appeared to improve in a process that could be described as the "provision of a synthetic ego." The educational therapist, it seems, patiently built a useful and usable prototype of ego functions for the student by building a stage for time and place to unfold. Through the boundaries of his physical self, the reality of his psychological self and that of others, he learned to distinguish his inner voice from outer voices, and by remembering and perceiving, ego functions were rehearsed. While the therapist "lends" an ego temporarily to a neurotic child, the educational therapist appears to "provide" an ego. Such an ego is functioning; though more rigid, less flexible, less able to extrapolate or to create novelty than a full ego, it serves its master in its performance by greatly improving his daily life and allowing him to ask for and utilize help in cruising over strange new territories. This *synthetic ego* equips the formerly helpless with routine living, providing a narrow but important range of coping devices.

At the same time, the task planning, the building of sequential time structures by completed and evaluated tasks, creates an image of the pupil as a "maker"—one who plans, does, and evaluates. The sequence of what comes next, what is expected, how it was done and that it is done, is used consistently like the song of the seasons. His stature as an autonomous and industrious human being emerges from these experiences.

What teacher and learner experience in this reality context differentiates the psychotherapeutic experience from educational therapy; while psychotherapy deals with fantasy on an output basis, educational therapy labels reality and fantasy as such, and provides reality congruence. The coping with the real world is the lodestone of educational therapy; even in terms of curriculum selection, educational therapy picks out the themes of mastery through knowledge, the power of understanding and of doing.

Thus, when students become rampant dinosaur scholars, cave maniacs, or horse expert's experts, these obvious preoccupations with intrapsychic content are used at their face-value as vehicles for learning. While the psychotherapist would deal with the meaning of the symbolism, the educational therapist utilizes these preoccupations to *enrich the evolving coping self of the student through his perceptual and cognitive mastery of the subject matter.* He would use such context to practice perceptual sorting, storage and retrieval, sequencing and conceptual strategies, all the while focusing on strengthening the capacity of the ego in fulfilling these roles.

As the dysfunctional student resorts to academic means to harness his fantasies, he has crossed over into the mainstream of functional learning. He, like his functioning peers, uses learning to tame the disordered turmoil of his inner life, to master his world through sequence and representation by symbols which he controls. Here, the student and his educational therapist have come to the crossroads where mankind's need to learn has sent them, where knowledge orders the universe and grants power over the forces of chaos.

EGO SYNTHESIS: A PSYCHOEDUCATIONAL PROCESS

Ego synthesis is the result of a psychoeducational process designed to improve the repertoire and behavioral integration of ego-dysfunctional children. This process involves a *cluster* of strategies, chosen to develop more stable and usable ego functions. In the absence of the natural emergence of ego functions, the ego-synthetic strategies of an educational therapist are designed to provide a "synthetic" set of behaviors enabling the dysfunctional child to navigate more appropriately and successfully. Ego functions can be seen as the helmsmen of the organism, steering a safe course based on past experience and present information. Without them, the organism tends to flounder in a maze of uncertainty and inappropriate responses. With the help of such acquired ego functions, the organism will cope better in the perceptual, cognitive, and social domains, seemingly steering a safer course.

The indispensable basis for functional coping is the availability of an ongoing self, consciously located in a space-time continuum. Such a self seems to work somewhat like a gyroscope providing a moving but continuing and clearly directional center from which sameness and change, action and inaction, the other, and the I, can be derived, providing a zero point from which directions can be plotted.

The process of ego synthesis may be visualized as involving strategies aimed at developing the following self-aspects: the *body self,* the *image self,* and the *executive self* or the experiencing, judging, and reacting self. While these aspects of the self are never discrete, they can be examined separately for purposes of this discussion. Each of these manifestations of the self are bound into a time-space framework to achieve functional integration, as they require the anchors of space and time.

This process is designed for the management of children whose ego impairment appears to be based on lags in developmental acquisitions or on distortions of functions that have already been acquired. However, equating ego dysfunction in children with that occurring in adolescents or adults may lead to erroneous conclusions. Because of the developmental aspects of childhood, management strategies must always include a patient waiting for functions to emerge as well as much education rather than re-education, growth as well as therapy.

The goal for a child, of course, must be the normalization of his developmental potential by providing capacities necessary for his independent further adequate growth. Such growth must encompass the input and output functions of appropriate information and communication skills. Thus, the goal of ego synthesis is the establishment of a clear sense of self which has stability and continuity, is possessed of a capacity to process information realistically, and can originate action in an appropriate manner. The child needs a zero-coordinate to know *who* he is, and *when* he is, and *where* he is.

The educational therapist mediates this process through modeling and rehearsal. He functions as a role model by being clear, open, able to permit success and failure, risk change, allow sameness, ask for and utilize and give feedback, all in a helpful, ego-enhancing and growth-promoting manner. While behaving in this manner, the educational therapist must also continuously set up situations in such a manner that the child has to actively rehearse ego-synthetic behaviors.

Thus, the therapist, to be successful, must possess the capacity to be clear and congruent about his own identity and consistently take clear responsibility for all his intentions and actions. Clarity and congruence in communication with severely dysfunctional children demand communication behaviors that would perhaps be considered redundant in normal social or educational intercourse.

Clear use of pronouns, the use of "I" as "I" and "we" only when collective "we" is denoted, is one example of the specific congruence required. The ascribing of action to inanimate objects or states, such as the "it occurs to me" when "I think" is meant, tends to further mystify a child whose reality sense is already impaired. Gestures and words must be congruent, *both* agreeing with the intended message.

Such almost pedantic compliance with clarity and congruence is quite difficult to carry off at first, but after some practice becomes second nature to the educational therapist. This apparently rapid shift in a basic communication style is facilitated by the strong positive reinforcement received from the child as his improved communication rewards the educational therapist for his effort to master clarity and congruence in his communication.

The clarity and congruence presented by the educational therapist is the basis for the synthesis of a clear, stable, and knowable physical self for the child. The educational therapist's self is delineated by his invariant appropriate use of pronouns to indicate the *actor* and *acted upon,* by establishing the speaker and the respondent, by clarifying the originator of a request, the request itself, and the person from whom such a request is made. As the therapist's self is thus delineated, the child's self, too, takes clearer shape.

The hallowed "Let 'us' now do 'our' spelling!" is the prime example of noncongruent requests that must be eliminated in the communication scheme with a dysfunctional child (hopefully, also with functional individuals). The role identification and role assignment of each communication segment must be unequivocally clear and true to intent. In this repeated transaction, the educational therapist fixes the focus of this self and thereby reinforces the development of all other "not-his selves"—such as the child's.

Developing the Body Self

The primacy of the body image in the progressive mental development of the child has been pointed out by many authorities. The possession of a clear and reality-based body image precedes all other learnings. The awareness of this physical self is initially a sensorimotor experience and thus in providing a body image for the dysfunctional child, the teaching experience, too, must be encoded in a sensorimotor modality. More mediate or derivative experiences regarding this physical self can only be derived from the vantage point of basic sensorimotor information about the physical self. Thus, the primacy of sensorimotor activity must be observed, only to be subsequently enlarged upon through more mediate processes such as art and language.

Physical self-definition is based on touching, seeing, hearing, smelling, and the kinesthetic or muscle senses. Observation of the problems of dysfunctional children in this area discloses not only their incomplete or erroneous perceptions, but also a lack of stability of these perceptions over a period of time or with regard to different locations. Therefore, these sensorimotor experiences with the physical self always must be presented in a time-space framework and must be the object of focal attention. In dealing with normal children we also deal with these phenomena; however, we make them peripheral to other attention foci as the normal child appears to require only minimal help in acquiring awareness in this area.

If the *body self* is to become the center of learning, direct focal attention must be centered on the sensorimotor component of this interaction. "You are holding your pencil while you write, your arm and shoulder guide your hand"—may be one way of providing such learning. A statement such as: "We write with our wrists relaxed," is a good example of a countertherapeutic approach.

Such sensorimotor emphasis on the body self of the child must be the invariable background music to all contacts with him. It is important to remember that often not only the whole-part relation is disturbed, but that sometimes the child is unaware of an entire segment of his body; or else his sense of boundaries and what is and what is not part of his self may be seriously impaired. Thus, what is clothing and what is skin, what is *his* clothing and what is still farther removed from his body must be learned; at the same time if these ideas are fuzzy, the boundaries between him and all others also must be checked out and firmed-in. The relation of the child's body and what he ingests and extrudes is also a part of this physical self-establishment. The confusion of body, of course, also encompasses the ingestive and eliminative products and require their distinction.

Making body image lessons time-and-situation related will solidify associational channels and provide bridges to more mediate experiences. For instance, handshaking can be an effective vehicle, when hands are shaken regularly on arrival or departure and clear focal attention is paid to this act. First, an awareness of "hand" as a part of an ongoing process is conveyed. One's hand becomes a part of the passage-and-change-of-time living experience, part of an invariable physical, affective, and social design. The invariance of what is touched, by whom it is touched, and in what social and affective context this touching occurs, anchors this hand to the context— a context which has the child's self as its invariant and constant factor.

Thus, this example shows the initial building of a stable referent with the child's physical self as the constant. Concurrently, many experiences of language accompany this one act, encoding the selfhood and belonging of the hand to its owner. Handprints, holding and dropping, catching and throwing, fingerpainting, touching, and stroking are all accessory experiences, provided they are handled again with clear identification of *my* hand, *your* hand, I give *you*, you give *me*, etc., thus locking in the physical entity to the experiencing self.

The awareness of "hand" thus becomes fused into the body image, as the connection of the hand-to-arm-to-shoulder is used in touching and art games, in looking at the mirror, photographs, and video playback and tapes.

The use of visual feedback combined with tactile and language experience appears to hasten the learning rate in this area. The use of Polaroid pictures, where the child can see himself a few moments after the picture was taken, while he is still within the social or experiential context in which the picture was obtained, helps him to apperceive his selfness within a given context. Frequent use of video instant playback and the replaying of recent tapes also serves this process well.

The part-experiences of the physical self need to be tied back to the whole body image incessantly. The "whole-body picture" serves this purpose well.

The *whole-body picture* is presented as an example of one major strategy for the establishment of the physical sense of self; however, the psychosocial aspects of selfhood are also part of this experience. The reference to the physical self refers to a predominance of such physical aspects in the awareness, so that a mature sense of self is anchored in the totality of experience.

Piaget's exposition postulates that the primacy of sensorimotor knowledge of the self precede the preoperational and operational aspects of self-awareness. Only the preoperational stage of awareness of self permits some sense of constancy of the self: for example, "me today" and "me tomorrow" and "me awake" and "me asleep," "me at school," and "me at home"; and only the attainment of the operational stage permits effective role-taking to allow empathy and thereby an insight into the feeling world of others.

The whole-body picture not only provides an intensive ongoing experience of the physical self of the pupil but also deals with this self as it introduces the concept of nonself and the other. This exercise explores not only the "I" and the "not I" but also the "I" and the "you."

Stable, ongoing, and predictable physical body boundaries help the ego-dysfunctional child to represent this selfness and anchor the "I" to a known, palpable, measurable, and retrievable entity. This entity is the child's body—the whole as well as the sum of its parts.

While we do not know why some individuals fail to develop such a stable sense of self or why some individuals—insidiously, at times, suddenly at others—lose this sense, we find that most children with such deficits can be helped to develop a sense of fitting body whole-ness which then serves them as the referent "I." The ability to use the pronoun "I" correctly—referring to one's self and not to a repe-titious echolalic imitation of another speaker—always occurs at a time when other coping ego functions appear in the child's behav-ioral repertoire as he gives up referring to himself as "he" or "she."

The whole-body picture is based on a representation of the child by a picture of his whole body, produced by tracing his outlines, as the educational therapist touches, names, relates parts to whole, and gives constant opportunities for consensual validation of the body outlines and characteristics. The consensual validations are provided both in an intersensory and in an interpersonal manner. The child is asked to touch, to look, to find the part in his mirror-image, on a photo of himself as well as on the therapist and other children and adults in his environment. We see this mirroring re-hearsal in many mother-child games where they probably serve an analogous function of anchoring the I and You, *your* body, and *my* body, into the developing infant's consciousness.

A cutting out of the body picture appears to assist the establish-ment of an awareness of body boundaries. Some children become very anxious about cuts being made into this outline, suggesting that they feel strongly identified with this image. At the same time, a gentle clarity about these boundaries seems to enhance a sense of wholeness and separateness for the child. Like the story, "when I was a baby," the story "how we made your picture," repeating and rehearsing the steps, appears to revalidate and strengthen this self-experience. Coloring or painting the image, letting the child adorn it, providing detail important to him, and allowing him to choose a place to keep it, and to keep it whatever length of time he "needs" it kept there, are important parts of this exercise. Again, how this image is "treated," the care and respect invested, will result in varying results—at its best, a sense of wholeness with caring and concern.

Developing the Image Self

Based upon a stable awareness of and continuity of the body self in space and time, the *image self* becomes elaborated in the context of many self-validating experiences. The beginning persona of the child develops in a context of mutually shared information about the unique attributes of each individual taking in the transaction. Such attributions tend to create an image that can serve as a known focus, or a self which is "me" and another self which is "you," and thus provide clearer images of roles and expectations based upon shared knowledge. This process, too, requires a temporal-spatial locking in to create the stability of continuity and sequence. Again, as in the development of the body self, focal attention must be given to these messages about the self.

Making identity a focal point of the "lesson," day after day, month after month, develops a usable body of information for the child, which slowly seems to coalesce into an image of an identifiable self. This emerging self serves him to define himself against others and provides him with a center to serve him for the reception and working-through of experiences.

While the "whole-body picture" is a prime example of a strategy to develop the physical self, exercises such as *The Book About Me* enhance the establishment of the image self. The development of an ongoing self with attributes, values, characteristics, a being in time, and a being in space helps the floundering ego-dysfunctional child to become anchored in an ongoing selfhood. His name and address, his age, the name of the place where the school is, the name of one's teacher, the names of one's peers, one's birthday date, color of hair, the name of one's pet—all these are aspects of self-ness—descriptions of that unique person, who alone is the possessor of all these characteristics. From the liking of ice cream cones to not liking to have one's face washed, the individuation, this being a certain person, becomes reinforced.

The educational therapist delineates the I from the non-I by often comparing the characteristics of peers, the therapist, and others, so that the being-one-self and others-being-their-own-selves becomes a motif of this learning task. Again, as in the exercises building the physical self, repetition and locking the experiences into temporal and spatial sequences increase their effectiveness and enhance the result.

It may sound exaggerated to suggest that, for instance, even in the early stages, identity book work be scheduled following some invariant temporal break in the day and that it be held at a set place in the instructional space. Yet, such locking of events into time and place further stabilizes the experience and potentiates the learning. To understand the rationale for this, it may help to visualize the ego-dysfunctional child as a person who has received some pathfinding direction, but who does not know where that path might begin. His physical and psychic self, albeit a synthetic one, provides him with such a starting point from which he can be shown further paths and from where we hope he will eventually find some of his own directions.

The pronoun-congruence, the emphasis on always using "I," "you," "we," and "they," and *always using them appropriately* cannot be overemphasized. The modeling of this selfness, with continuous rehearsal, facilitates not only congruent use, but apparently even a more congruent understanding of the I and You.

The development of an image self suggests the possession of an inner image or representation of the self. Such a representation presupposes some continuity in time and the ability to summon up an image, of having to have an image that can be called upon when needed. Thus, a sequential continuity, a self-sameness, must be available. Mediate processes, art and language, the innumerable products of the individual, and the continuities in the life experience, are all necessary for the establishment of such an image. Without such an image, first derived from a sense of physical being and then from an awareness of psychic continuity, no executive ego can emerge.

Developing the Executive Self

The possession of a fully executive self is the hallmark of a healthy mature personality. When we speak of the development of such an executive self in severely dysfunctional children, we refer to the growth gradient, or the direction in which we point our strategies. Yet, the beginnings of executive ego functions are discernible in successfully managed dysfunctional children.

The executive self becomes operational in the process of feedback, reflection, and empathic communication. As the physical self is built through the sensorimotor experience, the image self in the congruent use of verbal and nonverbal information about the attributes of the self, the executive self becomes operational through awareness of feelings and needs, pleasures and pains, anticipation and reminiscences. But most of all through volition the feeling of self grows in a process of temporal experiences, of becoming aware of feelings attendant to events, and of learning to monitor and perceive such feelings in the self and in the other. Here the educational therapist must suggest rather than teach, surmise rather than know, suspect rather than question.

The self cannot be "known." No one can read the mind of another, but one can surmise, guess, and suggest, that a person may feel unhappy about a loss, hurt by pain, or angry at being thwarted, joyous, grateful, or happy. One can patiently suggest that each child share his feelings with another, and one can enhance the relevance of this by helping guide the consequent behavior. If Johnny, indeed, feels hurt by a certain action, Johnny needs to be asked to tell this to the perpetrator and to ask him to desist. In this context, feelings then become knowable, communicable, and the basis for understandable actions. In this pragmatic manner, ego-dysfunctional children enter a world where feeling, action, and life experience converge.

While this is a highly concrete way by which to enter the world of feelings—a world that is considered by many of us as being most subtle and elusive—yet, "taught" this way, even severely ego-dysfunctional children appear to be able to enter, at least in a limited fashion, by making feelings a basis for behavioral responses, and highly appropriate responses at that.

In nurturing the executive functions of the self, both a sense of the passage of time and of the autonomy and potency of the self are necessary. It is in this executive self where the functions of making, changing, and causing reside. The sense of power, that it matters what I do, that it matters how I select my information, and what I do about it is important. Thus, the educational therapist will ask the child: "What did . . . say? What do *you* want to do about it?"; ". . . did not like what you did—what do *you* want to do about it?" Throughout, the child must be given true freedom to act if asked to choose an action, or told what to do if he does not have a choice of action.

This stage is of the most critical developmental period in the process of ego synthesis, as any failure of this nascent process of autonomous decision and action may seriously damage the child's tender new self-system. Great honesty and candor, great clarity of purpose, and an ability to risk regardless of personal comfort are required from the educational therapist. He must be prepared to face pain, fear, anger, and separation honestly, so that the child may experience the reality of these aspects of the human condition. Only if he can become part of a system where these aspects are out in the open and made accessible through a trusted and known other can he test reality for himself and hopefully find it safe enough to remain there.

Somewhere in this region of self-growth, the borderline between a functional ego that can continue to grow and that of a synthetic crutch-like ego exists. When we begin to work with a child, we never know where his growth limits may lie. Yet only the actual exploration of his limits will provide the answer to this question.

Ego synthesis involves strategies to provide for the development of *a stable body self, an image self, and an executive self.*

These three basic ego-synthetic processes: the building of a body self, an image self, and an executive self represent the hub of effective educational therapy with severely dysfunctional children.

The establishment of a working self in these three parameters rests on the concurrent establishment of a sense of time and space. The need for the maintenance of a sameness which is so characteristic of many dysfunctional children is possibly based on their limited spatiotemporal repertoire, and therefore a feeling of safety in the absence of change. By providing additional clear spatiotemporal benchmarks, the child becomes freer to choose, to change direction through actions, as his more stable self provides the continuity that only perseveration or self-stimulation could generate before.

The spatiotemporal framework is best provided by first using the basic entrance and exit point as well as the physiological bench-marks of food, sleep, and elimination. Doing certain things in certain places at given times provides such visible, memorable time and space stations; at the same time, in order to derive the necessary awareness of continuity and sequence, constant reflection is needed on "what happened before," "what will happen next," "what happened yesterday," "next week," "before snack," "where do we eat," "where are we going," "after you get up from rest." These reminiscences and preparatory rehearsals of spaces and times must be tied back into the self-space of the child. The touching, the remembering of feelings good and bad, the remembering what each person did, said, ate, or wore, builds such spatiotemporal informational sequences that tend to merge remembering, anticipating, and responding into a more stable self.

The emergent synthetic self in the dysfunctional child appears as a very fragile and tenuous structure: serving him well one time, lacking effectiveness at others, now being at the command of the child and now requiring the therapist's active initiation. Yet, these new ego functions are the indispensable foundation for socioemotional autonomy. Thus, even if they are fragmented and sporadic, when available and operant they are the essence of the child's self so that each time they do emerge some functional potency is possible. In addition, it appears that each such event creates certain reinforcing interactions between the child and his environment and thereby increases further occurrences. Thus, each act of selfhood carries the seed of enhanced ego functions.

THE THERAPEUTIC CURRICULUM AND
CURRICULAR THERAPY

Curriculum, "that-which-runs," provides the delivery system for education, delivering both content and process. *Content* represents the active ingredient or theme, *process* the behavioral function or teaching activity needed for learning.

Understanding of curricular content and process is based on an awareness of the ego-dysfunctional pupil as one who requires knowledge of the story as well as the techniques of his civilization presented in a form syntonic with his personal needs and wants.

Content, or *what* the curriculum contributes is the proper concern of the *therapeutic curriculum*; process or *how* the curriculum interacts with the learner's needs is the proper concern of *curricular therapy*. Thus, the therapeutic curriculum deals with segments of information in terms of students' intrapersonal needs. Curricular therapy, on the other hand, concerns the application of behavioral processes which develop skills based on interpersonal experiences between teacher and learner.

The content provided by the therapeutic curriculum might be seen as directly filling intrapsychic needs, providing psychic energy through direct information, by closing gaps, by cushioning tensions, and by answering questions. Curricular therapy also creates intrapsychic changes; however, these are achieved in an indirect manner through the increase of skill-coping on the one hand, and through those interpersonal strategies employed in the teaching process which provide ego enhancement through the experience of a more favorable or benign interaction both with people and information. Thus change occurs not only by ultimate outcome, but by the roads traveled to get there.

The pupil's need structure on the one hand and the curricular products and processes on the other must be weighed in terms of their mutual interaction to reach an optimal level of educational therapy. *What* is to be taught, *how* it is to be taught, and *when* this is to be taught, are essential decisions.

Pupil needs are based on factors such as ego strength, ego continuity, and ego stability, and the character and style of the coping behavior; the pupil's experiential history, communication style and resources, and his socioemotional status with special consideration of his unique predilections and preoccupations must be considered. The search for an appropriate therapeutic curriculum for a given pupil must start with an analysis of both the pupil's general and special needs and interests. Curricular inputs, or perhaps better, the modes of input, are determined by this assessment. Cooking might be taught to all students of a certain age, but teaching cooking to a specific pupil to illustrate ways of gaining autonomous satisfactions of overwhelming oral needs is an example of a therapeutic curriculum choice. Thus both ongoing as well as situational interests and concerns must be harnessed.

In assessing basic pupil needs, the following intrapsychic and intrapersonal areas must be examined in terms of *experiences* and *I-statements:*

(1) The need for *self-esteem, self-enhancement,* and *self-validation.* These are paramount needs. For this reason, the curriculum must provide chances for constant positive self-definition through coping, feedback for such coping, and some demonstrable closure or, in other words, it must always contain an opportunity for meaningful achievement—or, in the educational vernacular, "provide a success experience."

(2) The need for *environmental mastery* through *knowing* about the environment. This ranges from an awareness of time and space, selfhood and otherhood, from the here and now, to historical and geographical knowledge of time and space in a wider world. The greater the ego dysfunction of the pupil, the greater his needfulness for growth in the time-space dimension.

(3) The need for *safety and survival.* This can be met through skills development and knowledge involvement in areas such as the maintenance of health, self-help, and survival, as well as by many other aspects of science, as science represents the technology of mastery of the "real" world.

(4) A need for *integrative experiences.* These build the self and increase and deepen the knowledge and perceptions about the self and others, thus creating greater sensitivity and autonomy through exposure to feelings in both verbal and nonverbal encounters.

Curricula that pursue these goals satisfy basic ego needs and thereby improve general ego function.

Curricular therapy, based on a prior assessment of functional needs of the student, leads not only to growth from a gain in self-esteem as functional capacity increases, but also to specific remediations as information processing improves. The pupil will then see himself as a more potent individual—potent not only as "one who *can,*" but also as one who *"knows."*

The literature of academic therapy deals with the functional needs on which curricular therapy is based; therefore only a few examples will be cited here briefly. These areas may involve sensorimotor, perceptual, conceptual, interpersonal, and communication components. As curricular therapy is based on interpersonal contact, it can lay another foundation for the development of greater autonomy and a clearer sense of self. Curriculum that enhances sensorimotor skills is only thought of as programmed or specialized material, such as the Frostig or Dubnoff series. However, it is often forgotten that *all* activities have sensorimotor components; when provided, such training includes specific practice and feedback focused on this objective and it *ipso facto* becomes a specialized training exercise.

Frequently, the academic therapist must develop such special foci necessary for sensorimotor training. As background noise is to language, sensorimotor components are embedded in all educational experience. They must be lifted out from their background position and be brought into the foreground of consciousness. The educational therapist who intends to maximize sensorimotor learning must therefore lift the sensorimotor components out from the task at hand, and in a planned, prescriptive manner boost them into the primary teaching-learning focus. For instance, if handwriting is to be taught, attention must shift from the written word, its spelling, phonetic characteristics, or meanings, to the motor configuration, which in other teaching contexts would be only a background phenomenon. Incidentally, care must be taken that the stimuli used do not have such strong foreground value as to interfere with attention to the background. For instance, a child with fears of injury may not be able to attend to the word "blood" or "accident" when used for a handwriting improvement exercise.

Even in a child with a very severe handwriting difficulty, other learning objectives often must take precedence, ranging from psychic survival to a need for greater creativity or communication skill. At such times, the motor component of handwriting would not be focused on, in order to free effort for other chosen objectives. At other times, a priority of motor training may be necessary or appropriate and the sensory or motor components of that exercise can then become the primary learning focus.

In curricular therapy, the therapist's attention must monitor the task factor loadings of a learning activity as well as the need state of the pupil by continuously shifting his focus of attention from one to the other. Here, the educational therapist performs like a conductor bringing out the different instruments of his orchestra, and letting various sections carry the tune; at one point the motor component, at some other the auditory, visual, or the conceptual loading of a task, will carry the teaching melody. Sometimes, as in the orchestra, a number of parts can be combined in a synergistic maneuver for heightened effect. The mobilization of the motor system, for instance, can increase attention and memory, so that asking the pupil to get up, write on the board, or raise his hand improves the entire response by mobilizing his orienting reflex and attention, and providing kinesthetic and proprioceptive reinforcement.

The interpersonal aspects of the curriculum involve not only motivation but also reinforce with *strategy*: for instance, the amount of voice and gesture contact, how close or intimate, how far or distant the pupil and the therapist should be from each other at any given time. Such decisions are based both on the needs of the student and on the specific objectives of a given curricular offering. When greater independence and self-motivation is the learning goal, the closeness and interaction of the therapist and the student must be planned differently from a learning objective that must aim at close contact or perhaps even intrusion into the pupil's perceptual and life spaces.

Sometimes, at the outset of teaching severely dysfunctional children, a constant, almost intrusive presence of the educational therapist is required. The withdrawal defenses of the severely dysfunctional, especially the autistic child, actively defend against interaction. These defenses must be breached before meaningful learning can occur. On the other hand, when a student is enmeshed in a power struggle with his environment, he will only become more immobilized in his learning if the educational therapist were to exude an intrusive presence. Sometimes, such intrusion might consist of a need for eye contact with the pupil, or for appropriate language, or for an appropriate "time and place" for certain activities, or may require the pupil to vaguely acknowledge the teacher's presence. Thus, the teacher's self must be constantly used in meaningful interaction, and becomes a part of the curricular unit. What is important, however, is that the educational therapist have both a didactic and an interpersonal objective for every lesson or time sequence, defining his own role, as part of the learning transaction involves not only motivation but also reinforcement strategies.

Due to phobic or other intrapsychic interferences, severely dysfunctional pupils may arrive at magic solutions or may even be unable to use certain learning processes because of idiosyncratic distortions of communication and cognition. Therefore, the *what to say,* the *how to get there,* the *modeling* of *steps of reasoning,* of *information gathering* or *information compiling, conclusion making* and *communication* is important. Since cognition uses pattern-comparison and recognition, the scanning for likenesses and differences, for partial or complete matches, and for decisions regarding the state of a given comparison is a major part of cognitive growth. Modeling these processes and performing these cognitive tasks in front of and *with* the pupil are essential steps. The educational therapist must think "in public" so that the pupil may observe and imitate him.

Increasing the pupil's autonomy is one of the central goals of curricular therapy. Growth in autonomy is attained through appropriate interaction between the experiencing person and his environment. To gain autonomy, one must perceive in a predictable manner, experience constancy of objects and persons, and know boundaries between the inner self, the outer boundaries of the self, and the world beyond the self. Should the pupil's autonomy be tenuous, curricular therapy must attend to this objective in *every* learning activity and must include it in both the selection of learning stimuli as well as in the total ongoing teacher-learner interaction. When basic autonomy is impaired, the pupil will be enthralled by infantile omnipotence. This fortress must be breached before he can command reality-focused attention needed to master further meaningful learning. This autonomy increases as he interacts with a truly autonomous educational therapist and as his mastery of feeling, perceiving, and knowing grows. The pupil's autonomy grows as more learning functions become available to him and as he acquires additional reality-oriented information-processing skills, developed with an increasingly more reality-based relationship with his teacher. His volitional integrity in utilizing his new skills is the capstone for his autonomy.

To discover appropriate themes the therapist searching for a therapeutic curriculum must have access to the entire world of knowledge. The arts and sciences derive from the human need to cope with both the external and internal world. The arts make coping with the internal, psychic, and interpersonal tasks possible, the sciences help man to survive in the external physical world. The dysfunctional student needs these all-human themes to create a world in which he can cope more adequately. The therapeutic curriculum provides knowledge for coping; the educational therapist must discover his pupil's specific coping needs and then deliver the necessary content to fill these needs.

When fear of disaster, or intrusive fantasies about monsters and witches, earthquakes or tornadoes, death or destruction enthrall a pupil, a sharing exchange about this world will make it less threatening by being shared with somebody who seems less threatened by its landscape so his panic may subside. At the same time, learning about, and thereby cognitively handling these materials, provides one form of mastery over dreaded themes.

An equally important though different aspect of the thematic use of curriculum is that of desensitization. The material cools by working through, and working out, and thus becomes ego syntonic. In the cool light of school performance, a world of overwhelming inner fantasy if shared, coped with, and illuminated by knowledge, becomes attenuated, the urgency and frighteningness of such material diminishes.

In this sense, the study of topics such as caves, volcanoes, dinosaurs, electric light circuits, or any number of other preoccupations helps reduce, dissolve, or solve certain conflicts.

At the same time, the interpersonal sharing of knowledge with a trusted person who is obviously not being overwhelmed by something that appears overwhelming to the pupil provides growth in two directions: one by the incorporation of previously unincorporable material, and two, through the establishment of a new and safe experience within a helping relationship. Here, *trust, autonomy,* and *industry*, Erikson's three basic epigenetic experiences, are enhanced.

In conclusion, here are some examples of the application of themata and processes, of content and skill, or of a therapeutic curriculum and curricular therapy.

The "loaded" field of mathematics provides good examples of the different ways to view curriculum. However, there are some dysfunctional children who take refuge in the world of numbers to protect themselves from contact with the world of people and events, which they see as threatening, even possibly lethal. We also know students who had to eliminate the world of numbers from their own reality to defend themselves against the threat of some overwhelming danger that appeared to lurk within this world of numbers; thus, to them, not-learning-mathematics is a way of maintaining security. Such different ways of behaving vis-a-vis mathematics demand different appropriate approaches.

The student who is totally immersed in a world of numbers can be presented with a number world that slowly becomes populated: first by objects, then by animals, and much later by some people. Later, concepts of a world of numbers which is helpful to all people can be added. Thus, his world is widened and slowly becomes a safer world for him. For instance, biostatistics aiding health, the role of numbers in creating food supplies or some other gratifications will expand and humanize his world. Here, curriculum is used as a therapeutic agent.

The youngster who had to defend himself against mathematics as being dangerous to him can be helped to conquer and gain a more comprehensive world through a very careful and gentle introduction to numerical information. If, for instance, such a pupil is interested in a pet, the counting or measuring of food for his pet, or the keeping of numerical records about his charge can be effective. Thus, he may enter a world previously closed to him, using his own concerns as the key.

Often some students feel panic with concepts such as subtraction and division because of their association with destructive or destroying phenomena. The student can be desensitized and can gain a capacity to utilize that part of his external world that he previously had to avoid. If the educational therapist is aware of such a defense against part of a learning or informational system, the use of relabeling and subtle reinforcement through knowledge gain is required.

A final example of such curricular uses would be the enhancement of the self-concept by using a body-image focus. For intact learning skills, an intact body image is necessary. Our body image is the baseline and point zero of our personal world. The nature of this body image determines where we locate this zero point in the external universe, and how we delineate this external universe we created from our own personal universe. Thus, teaching about the body image touches the basic coordinates of time, space, and self: the awareness of the self as a living, experiencing, and coping individual.

Therefore, a whole-body-self drawing performed with the aid of the educational therapist represents the core curriculum par excellence. Through tracing, coloring, and labeling the experience of the pupil's self becomes validated; self-touch, mirror check, and touching the other person give concrete and socialized information; naming and describing add language to the "lesson." Included in this basic learning experience are sensory motor components such as tracing, looking and touching, finding the whole-part relationship, and relational or interpersonal components through close interaction between the self and the "other": the educational therapist. Here the educational therapist becomes an important interpreter of the physical self of the student.

In a thematic and communicative context, the fears and concerns about health, life, death, survival, and life functions must be dealt with. Such themes should be covered as: how the body works, how it heals itself, how it grows and changes, how it can counter physical and psychic insults, and how and what feelings develop both from within the body and in response to other people. Such a curriculum then deals with and augments the substance of the pupil's human selfhood.

In the foregoing section we have discussed some new ways to view curriculum for students requiring educational therapy. A therapeutic curriculum alleviates distress and promotes growth through themata that aid cognitive and affective mastery of the pupil's world. Curricular therapy, on the other hand, comprises strategies that augment the pupil's learning skills, increasing his capabilities to obtain and to use information necessary to cope with his environment. Both curricular therapy and the therapeutic curriculum involve a relationship between pupil and teacher, thereby invoking human relatedness for human growth.

TYING AND UNTYING: THE SOCIOEMOTIONAL DIMENSION

The dysfunctional child invariably experiences inappropriate interpersonal encounters, either based directly on his deficiencies and malfunctions or as the result of inadequate or incongruent feedback. His dealings with adults *and* with his peers merit both scrutiny and assistance.

The setting of his social encounters must provide graded opportunities for social experience for rehearsal allowing feedback and correction, and for a variety of healthy role models. For the young school-age dysfunctional child, an opportunity to relate to children of preschool age within a nursery school setting is the environment of choice. Such a preschool environment provides peers with simpler play and social patterns and allows the dysfunctional child some social equality and permission to operate at a parallel and presocial play level. The physical setting provides for much large muscle play, simple motor activities, and spaces that allow much free exploring, grouping, and regrouping in a large variety of ways.

When moving in and out of simpler social relationships is possible, social growth which proceeds by fits of progression, standstills, and regressions can pace itself more securely. The dysfunctional child can move forward or regress and is allowed many rehearsals depending on his particular needs and stress factors, as well as moods of the day. He is thus more likely to find positively reinforcing experiences, allowing him to continue his social experimentation. While the setting provides such permission, the availability of watchful and skilled adult support and adult intervention is needed to ensure steady progress in this area.

Socialization can be induced in such a way that the child can pace himself, going forward and backward, being solitary and then again gregarious, having younger and older, stronger and weaker individuals to choose from. Settings that contain all these options, preferably simultaneously, will create a life-space that provides the requisite social learning opportunities. In such a life-space, the educational therapist functions like a stage director at rehearsal, blocking out encounters, suggesting ways in which feelings and intentions can be expressed, and helping with meaningful responses. Like the stage director, the therapist also comments by summing up, by reinforcing desired scenes, and by preparing for change and better replay of the less effective ones. He will provide for appropriate use of rehearsal time so that the cast may reach the real job of the impending performance in good time.

As the locus of selfhood is a product of the individual's experience with the other, the educational therapist and the other adult helpers will expend much of their watchfulness on all the social transactions of the dysfunctional child. As his selfhood emerges, his ability to receive and to send congruent messages about the self must be consistently monitored and assisted; such assistance implies attempts to clarify feelings, make messages conform with intentions, and aids the child to learn to ask for clarification and to confirm or disconfirm messages, depending on their appropriateness or effectiveness. At certain times, this becomes very time-consuming, almost as laborious as taking a poem apart to find images, meter, and symbols. The freshness and spontaneity of encounters go by the board—yet only within such painstaking analysis can the essence of each encounter be demonstrated. The dysfunctional child who had not been able to learn fitting social skills through sheer empathic experience appears to be able to acquire them, albeit the hard way, through analysis, demonstration, and rehearsal. At times the educational therapist functions as the child's alter ego—saying or acting for him, checking back as to whether this represented the intended action, and openly evaluating each outcome.

When acting as such an *alter ego*, the educational therapist must be careful to let the pupil know that the therapist is acting in his stead, and to check whether his actions are congruent with the student's intent and whether the student will permit such a trial run on his behalf. The therapist asks: "May I tell John to give it back to you?"; "John *did* give it back—do you feel better now?" This is one way of summing up and of suggesting that the pupil himself try this approach next time. Suggestions, such as, "Perhaps if you tell him . . . he will stop!" is another way in which role modeling by the therapist may be used.

Again, it must always be clear that the therapist cannot ever read the pupil's mind, that he is a totally separate person, and can only speculate on how the pupil may feel. Therefore he *has* to check out *each* time whether his assumptions about the pupil's intentions, feelings, and perceptions are correct. He will never assert that a pupil is angry or sad, but will wonder whether he is, or share his perception that he may look as if he were feeling that way. Not only will this strengthen the mutual autonomy, but it will also stress the requirement for check-out, feedback, and for validation. If the desired outcome is to be the acquisition of independent, effective social skills, then feelings and congruent perceptions must be accepted, utilized, and responded to. The dysfunctional child must become more able to express these perceptions and feelings openly, and to use this clearer perceptiveness in reading others and in responding to their messages.

For instance, if a toy is taken from an apparently uncomplaining child, the therapist may say: "Did you want to give this to Barry now, or did you want to keep it?" "Oh, you wanted to keep it! Okay, then tell Barry you need it still!" "Can he have it later? If you think so, tell him he can have it when you are ready." Such encounters must be highly specific, perhaps even suggesting the exact time when the toy will be handed over. The therapist may give help by telling the other child how each of them feels about it, yet always making sure that the child's *real* feelings, and not the adult's hoped for or imagined idea gets expressed. Generosity, which the adult may hope for, is not the usual feeling; anger, envy, and impatience is. This must be expressed so that the confirmation of real feelings can become the basis of real socialization by an individual whose self is an actual part of the action. If it is hoped that such social learning will become internalized, usable in the future without the presence of the instigating adult, the child must get in touch with his real feelings so that he can develop ego-syntonic actions.

In our culture, where anger and fear between individuals often is suppressed or distorted, open admission of such feelings is rarely practiced. Unless legitimized as "righteous," anger must be masked. For the dysfunctional, even more than for the culturally functioning individual, such distinctions and distortions immobilize social growth. Therefore, in helping these children to become more practiced in social interactions, openness and congruence is required.

Toleration of behavior that is really intolerable is one such example of an antitherapeutic stance by adults in the child's environment. When behavior that is highly uncomfortable is tolerated for a while, ostensibly to spare the child from criticism, stopping it only when it is "too much" is most confusing and often injurious to the child; for when this finally occurs, the adult has already swallowed much anger and displeasure while he held back on his intervention. Thus the intervention *when* it is made, usually carries more anger and irritation than it would have contained at the outset. Unacceptable behavior—that is, behavior that is unacceptable to the caretaker—must be curbed or at least commented upon as soon as it occurs, so that the interaction between child and caretaker may be open, honest, and effectual.

All "double-binding" must be scrupulously avoided. We must not give choices that really are not choices, but where one choice is the desired and the other would have an actually undesired or unsanctioned outcome, we must direct firmly. Caretakers of the dysfunctional must be able to express disapproval and approval honestly, so that the dysfunctional child knows at all times where he stands. If disapproval becomes the predominant feeling, and, in spite of support of the caretaker the child's peculiar mode of acting continues to evoke such reaction, the two should be separated and another caretaker found. Neither dissembling nor constant negative feedback can promote positive social growth.

The administrative social climate, too, must model such congruent openness. When this is done, and it is necessary so to ensure the same kind of behavior vis-a-vis the children, it becomes quite clear how unused adults in our culture are to dealing openly and closely with issues. Often they will feel totally attacked or totally rejected when both praise and criticisms are shared directly, openly, and without hyperbole. In the language of adult convention, the expression of even one criticism may signify a total criticism, on the assumption that taking issue with one item is representative of the whole.

Our cultural framework assumes either total acceptance or total rejection. Thus if someone is to feel loved, he must wish for total acceptance; barring this, love or approval will not be assured. Again, with the precarious state of socialization of dysfunctional children, it is even more necessary that they experience *fractional* and *specific approval* or *disapproval,* hearing: "I like this"; "John does not like it when you kick him!"; "Betty liked it when you shared the cookie—she did not like it when you spat into her soup." Thus, appropriate and specific attributes *must* be commented upon giving continuous and clear feedback. The child, too, must be helped to give out such feedback, helping him to create a functioning social resonance so that he, too, can monitor his social environment and thereby grow in his social skills.

Thus the acquisition of socioemotional skills involves an ordering of relationships, or a tying and untying of human contacts. As in a play, the social-role functions comprise not only a coming together, a staying together, but also ways in which the protagonists take leave. The malfunctions of socialization as well as functional potency involve all three of these aspects. Perhaps the last, the untying or leave-taking, is fraught with some of the greatest hazards. It seems likely that for the dysfunctional the hazards inherent in separation may be tied into his poor self-image, his experiences with feeling unloved or reluctance for change, and his need for the preservation of sameness. This need for sameness may stem from many sources, such as his perceptual inconstancy, his need-fear orientation which tells him that he desperately needs other people who may not be always available to him, as well as struggles with some overpowering fantasies of destruction and of being destroyed. Whatever the source of the dysfunctional child's problem with separation, learning to experience and cope with separation is a major need.

Separation, separation anxiety, denial or fear of separating, and innumerable maneuvers to ritualize, minimize, or transform separations are also a part of all of us—functioning or not, adult or child. Managing these needs in others is particularly difficult because of the universality of profound feelings regarding leavetaking, death, separation, abandonment, and aloneness. To assist the dysfunctional child to cope with his awareness of leavetaking and the social management of leavetaking, we must level with our own concerns and problems in this area.

Each leavetaking must be open; preparation for it must be made and honestly expressed whether such leavetaking is temporary or permanent. This honesty toward even a single separation, allowing all available grief to be openly expressed, can go far in providing socioemotional growth. It seems as if such shared, open, fully experienced separation can provide some indispensable learning in being human. Even great grief, openly expressed, particularly if it concerns the tragic separateness of human beings, can provide a profound and ultimately healing experience. Through such pain a healthier, more open, autonomous, and stronger person emerges.

The educational therapist, in guiding the ties that symbolize human relatedness, provides the matrix for human relatedness: the ability to deal congruently with social givens, the ties of work and of play, the coming and going, the greeting and the leavetaking.

AWARENESS AND RESPONSIVENESS: SPACE AND TIME

The educational therapist must possess a high level of awareness if he is to involve himself in the continuous need assessment and interpersonal functions. His major tools are awareness and responsiveness to his own inner feelings, to the child's feelings, and to messages of space, time, and environment.

Such awareness and responsiveness are never fully attained but represent an ongoing process of getting in touch and remaining in touch with one's feelings of body and of mind. This skill is evanescent and elusive, constantly subject to needs for denial, rest, and noninvolvement; yet the discomfort of not being in touch, too, gnaws on the person with messages of nonfulfillment, of not having seen or heard, and the malaise of partial ignorance. The process of seeking and avoiding awareness is like that of the thermostat that opens the gate for heat when cold, and for cold when hot, oscillating with constant change. All of us have a number of available devices to monitor our awareness and to increase or decrease our responsiveness.

The prime indicator of our state of both being us and of being with others is our own body which *is* us. At all times our body reflects our feelings and our knowings about ourselves and in resonant response to others, in subtle tension, in fleeting fantasies, thoughts, moods, and feelings. We have the capacity to turn our awareness away from most of this, so much so that some of us even get quite seriously ill from tension illness before we hear the voice of our body, when we could have heard a very early twinge of warning. Our muscle system develops tension and tensions develop discomfort, pain, imbalance, and illness. Our visceral system changes the functioning of our heart, of our breathing, and our intestinal tract in many ways that say how things are changing. Feelings of sadness, joy, depression, anxiety, and apprehension force themselves through us, sometimes rapidly, often waiting to be stopped, picked up, and examined for the implied messages. Letting these awarenesses come into our consciousness, staying with them instead of turning them away as being trivial, unimportant, and not worth our attention, are ways in which we increase our awareness potential, thus becoming truly aware of both ourselves and others. Such awareness must precede all responsiveness and appropriate responding.

Perhaps we all should have "an awareness time" when we make room for a deeper experience of awareness; a time that is ours, that allows us to communicate with ourselves without the distraction of having to communicate with others; or, if we are in a difficult role, we need to be in touch and stay in touch with ourselves and with those expressions of ourselves that tell us what's with us and what's with others.

Awareness of the other is based on the "clear-channel reception" of our own awareness, because the information about where somebody else might be has to be transmitted to us through *our* self-awareness, mediated by the kind of response that the feelings coming from the other person invokes in us.

As we become more sensitive to the other and our own awareness, we can get in touch with many subtly expressed feelings as we tune in our responses. We will find that a sudden feeling of tearfulness in our head will signal sadness or tearfulness in the other person. A sudden tenseness in our neck muscles is a response, perhaps, to the tenseness in the other. Our well-tempered awareness becomes the dependable indicator of the feelings of those around us. Not only the sympathetic resonance, but also the unsympathetic nonresonance are valid indicators. Nonsympathetic nonresonance is the signal that tells us that we have just turned off the other. This is a highly significant signal asking us to search for the discomfort that the feelings

of the other person have evoked in us. Particularly after we have become a well-tempered resonator to the feelings of others, our need
to turn off and shut out indicates an emergency situation calling for
immediate active search-and-seizure of the missing link—the signal
we needed to turn away from.

Awareness training proceeds from a number of simple exercises, as
many training facilitators offer in awareness and sensitivity training.
These exercises are not difficult and are of a limited variety. But it
is important to realize that merely going through these exercises a
number of times will not create a state of instant cosmic awareness.
Rather, this process of gaining such awareness proceeds in slow, continued stages throughout a lifetime and without end. We must continue to practice getting in touch with our breathing, the feelings in
our muscles, the learning to let feelings persist and to permit their
experience, though they may be uncomfortable at times. We must
learn to clear our mind from interfering thoughts and develop that
most crucial skill, the ability to get in touch with whatever is interfering with our own awareness, so that we can become cognizant of
that which is preempting our feelings, our mind, and our body. For
it is this, whatever it is that preempts our attention, that constitutes
the central problem we are facing at that particular time. Dealing
with it or putting it where it does not overwhelm the rest of our
awareness capacities is probably the primary goal of awareness
training.

For those who have not experienced the traditional initial approach
in awareness training, the following exercises and experiences introduce awareness phenomena. Regulated deep breathing often introduces changes that aid in bringing an automatic process under conscious awareness. Such changes may be alternating nostril-breathing,
concentrating on the action of the diaphragm or the chest muscles,
lengthening or shortening inhalation or exhalation, holding or post-

poning breathing. Muscle awareness is based on self-report through increased concentration on certain muscle groups, both their tensing and relaxing. Feeling awareness is very often mediated by other experiences such as drawing, painting, sculpting, whistling, symbolic representation of feelings by body posture, or art expression. In each of these experiences automatic or otherwise not consciously noticed processes are forced into consciousness and thereby create available awareness through change. In this way, unconscious processes become conscious, open to examination and feedback.

The environment in which the pupil and teacher reside is a very complex one which often goes unexamined and unobserved. This is unfortunate, as *space* and its characteristics influence the process of mutual awareness and the outcome of the interaction in many important ways. Space, of course, is also a signal in itself. It is therefore highly desirable that we become more conversant with the data space present to us and also begin to structure and to change space to provide it in such a way that it will enhance the desired interaction.

Modern ethology has started to concern itself with the way in which space influences organisms and also the way in which organisms utilize space to influence their own feelings and their dealings with other individuals or species. The most important dimension in this respect is the degree of closeness ranging from skin-to-skin contact to infinite distance. The location of two bodies somewhere on this continuum expresses many feelings and carries many messages, from messages of support to messages of total abandonment, from messages of permissible or nonpermissible intrusion to messages of comfortable distance. The function of distance together with the function of speech and other auditory signals also will increase the clarity of understanding of messages over a given distance. The posi-

131

tioning of bodies in this space with respect to freedom of egress and approach, for instance, will help to facilitate or inhibit feelings of security, intimacy, threat, or repulsion.

In the exploratory phase of getting acquainted when partners are anxious about the safety of the encounter, blocking the exit or avenue for distancing can be extremely threatening. On the other hand, an encounter of supposed intimacy where at least one participant will position himself ready to escape carries a message of tentativeness, fear, and lack of trust.

The permission of freedom or lack of freedom of movement which is often indicated by the availability of a straight line between the organism and the potentially desired goal will tell the story of facilitation or inhibition of potential moves. In putting up a learning station or a classroom, the placement of the furniture in relation to the door, the placement of the teacher's and the pupils' station in relation to the accessibility of the exit or the entrance, the materials that we want the student to use and those we do not want him to utilize at a given time, can influence the interaction of teacher and student to a great degree.

Many of us have seemingly learned to disassociate ourselves consciously from the spaces we inhabit as we have had to operate in so many unsuitable and uncomfortable spaces in our lives. However, when we are involved in a helping process, it is important that we recapture some of these awarenesses and maybe even rehearse them in the space that we plan to use. Thus, we will get to know what we are saying with our space arrangement and can try and structure it in such a way that it will communicate and facilitate those goals which we have set for our interaction.

Besides the physical placement within this space, the participants in relation to each other and the props or furniture chosen, the size, the color, their richness, or poverty are also messages. It would be very desirable for educational therapists to "try on" their spaces for some time before using them with a pupil. Only after having learned and structured the space on the basis of that experience will they discover what messages this space sends and how they can become the servants of the teaching act.

In conclusion, we also must remain in touch with those messages which space sends out; perhaps by playing the role of a stage "director-designer" can we visualize how space is used to set up scenes, to facilitate or inhibit, to create feelings, illusion, and fantasies, or how to create a special reality from a bare space. A stage uses distance and height, color, light, and texture, and particularly the relationships in space between people and objects to tell the story. A reigning monarch will not sit on a low stool in a small room, rubbing shoulders with his subjects. A cornered man, driven by his conscience, will not be depicted in an open, light, soft-colored expanse. The educational therapist, like the stage director, will try to provide settings both animate and inanimate that are congruent with the intent and needs of all roles that make up his teaching situation and, as the playwright and director, he will also use time and timing to present the action.

Time has a number of dimensions in this interaction: a sense of *speed* in an adjustment to the time style of the pupil, a sense of *timing*, or a recognition that certain events require special moments in time to be effective, and also a sense of the appropriate *sequencing* for different tasks.

The speed style of a person, which is often different for varying activities, is one important dimension. Often dysfunctional people live at highly varying paces; honoring such pacing is necessary in order to obtain optimal attention and learning. At the same time, when such pacing violates the therapist's basic needs, this too should be communicated to the pupil and ways found where each member of this dyad can proceed at his own speed rather than languish in states of discomfort and frustration. The slowness of the passive-aggressive resister is one such speed and timing problem. If such slowness is banished from the interaction by openly "granting" choice of speed to the pupil, such distorted slowness tends to fade out rapidly; if such passively resisting slowness remains a battle-ground, slowness will, of course, be reinforced as a most successful weapon. Defensive and shoddy speed of a pupil who may be afraid to try hard and well, can be handled in a similar manner.

The life-rhythms of people, their good times and poor times, their alert times and their tired times, must be ascertained and utilized to their best advantage. Moments of receptiveness and times of turned-offness, too, need to be honored.

Pacing and sequence, however, are of special importance. In all teaching, allowing the hidden agenda to be cleared first, finishing content that is preoccupying before moving on, letting perseverative people close off their previous task, are all very important points. The therapist's full awareness must be tuned in to the pupil's time state and assess his readiness or unreadiness for a next step. At the same time, the sequence of material must proceed so that the more calming and quieting and also the more calm-requiring material will precede the more stimulating and active material; content that challenges strong emotion must not precede content that requires persistent, quiet, and attentive effort. A lesson on volcanoes should not precede a practice session in the addition of numbers, if turmoil, violence, and anxiety are provoked by the former, for it may well spill over to the latter.

An experiential lesson requiring large muscle action should not precede a quiet, mood-filled listening game. Yet this is done and will continue to be done, unless the therapist rehearses the emotional tone as well as the sequential plans of the intended lesson.

Responsiveness flows smoothly from full awareness. Video-playback and feedback from observers are helpful in sharpening responses; however, essentially responsiveness is the reverse side of the awareness coin. A receptive, feeling, sensitively aware person will respond from this inner sensitivity and make the "correct" response. The correct response is *that* communication which confirms the other in the feeling state he is currently experiencing and thus enables him to make his next move in a direction that is congruent with his being, allowing him to *be* and thus *grow in his being.*

Chapter 5
CASE ILLUSTRATIONS

The voice does not speak to me as it does to you. I am a man: you are only a grown-up child. One does not speak to a child as to a man. And a man does not listen and tremble in silence. He replies: he makes the Voice respect him: in the end he dictates what the Voice shall say.

—G. B. Shaw, *Back to Methuselah*

What are some of the changes that were observed, and how were they different from those observed in the school careers of other school children? To answer these questions, a few brief case histories of these students during their experiences under our psycho-educational management are reported. The student names are disguised to protect their anonymity. Their drawings are shown to illustrate the change in the experience of themselves as human beings and in their projections of their environment.

John: John was first seen at age three, referred for evaluation in preparation to placement in a hospital for the profoundly retarded. He was without any speech, limp, unable to care for himself in any manner, and spending his days shredding paper and angrily screaming. He would not stop his distress signals when a helping adult approached, seemed oblivious of them and would not calm down until the desired request was granted. He averted his gaze and appeared ignorant of his environment, except for twirling objects, and shredding paper endlessly to the understandable distress of his environment.

At age nine, John is joining a class for slow learners on a full-time basis; he has communicative speech which includes describing his feelings and guessing at the feelings of others, solid beginning academic work, an ability to play some games with children, and to form personal relationships with a few adults and children. This functioning world was created with John by a succession of three educational therapists who first "demanded" and later received attention, then "demanded" and received verbal responses, and finally "demanded" and received academic achievement. This "demanding" consisted of letting John experience a trusting relationship with the educational therapist, always focusing on John's being in a consensual world with her—sharing her perceptions, impressions, and feelings and constantly calling on John to experience

with her and share this experience if he so desired. The educational therapist stayed with John in a very basic world of simple sounds,
simple sights, simple touch, and basic feelings. The therapist always
tied all experience into the present world, explaining its immediate
antecedents, and preparing for the immediate next step. They at-
tempted to share the processes of her thought, the whys and
wherefores, her feelings about her experience, and she invited
John's awareness of his.

The first interaction with an adult by John occurred two months
after his therapist, a student, began daily work with him. It consisted of John's throwing a frisbee so that the therapist had to retrieve it. This act seemed to test her willingness to interact; this gesture was used by this educational therapist to validate interest and
relationship, but at the same time, to create a common space, cause
and effect, the you and the I, and the action and actor dimension.
The educational therapist would comment on *where* the frisbee
was, *when* she would pick it up, *what* the place looked like where
she found it, *who* had tossed it, and in a hundred ways bring the
shared cognitive reality into that relationship.

Echolalic language began one month after that frisbee game com
menced; communicative language, about four months later.

John's course was stormy, with ups and downs, progress and regress. However, after each regression, as progress resumed the previous phase appeared better established and consolidated. The call
upon the educational therapist's patience and inventiveness was
great, but she could ask for and get regular outside support.

Today John can ask for help, can indicate his off days and can
pace himself and his relationships. At the same time, when con-
fronted with a completely new situation, John may panic at first,

resume some of his mannerisms of toewalking, automatic speech, and seeming lack of relationship. His ego functions, but with a lack of spontaneous creativity which functioning children bring to novelty. However, his ego provides a sorting out of new stimuli, tying them to previously known experiences or ways of behaving, and thus John's ego can cope with novelty to some extent.

John uses his reading to cope with fear, anxiety, and distress; his reading words concern "vomiting," being "lost," monsters and separation; as he asks to learn these words, he appears more able to handle the situations or feelings referred to.

With John, learning and learning skills of a preschool and early school child provide the basic texture of his human development. They are not the "frills" or the cultural extra of development; they must provide the base on which John's coping and growth is built.

At the time of this writing, John is eleven years old. He has spent one year in a full-day class for educable mentally retarded pupils. He can perform the basic academic skills and is a member of his male social group. He has been able to be helpful with a new young student in his class, relating to him with some warmth and protection. He participated in a summer school and could give support to a very angry but panicked boy whose behavior John correctly labeled as fear. He was able to use this by showing this child the needlessness of some of these fears, and thereby helped him to cope.

For one year John had an hour a week of relationship therapy and later was able to share with his therapist some very personal statements about his feelings of terror and his fears about his world. He has asked the therapist at times to help him control his fears and to control some of his mannerisms, which he realizes get in the way of communicating—of "being heard."

JOHN

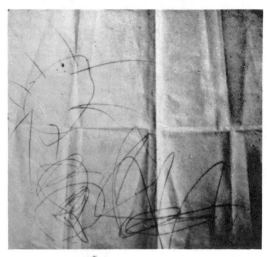

8 years 2 months

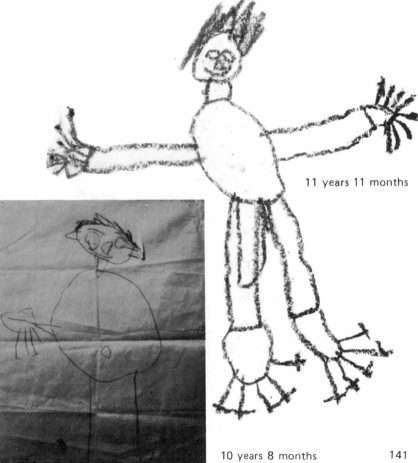

11 years 11 months

10 years 8 months   141

The development of John, who probably was our most dysfunctional child to begin with, is illustrated in the three drawings: his almost unrecognizable human figure at the age of 8 years 2 months where he was barely able to draw a face which he quickly covered with scribbles, his recognizable human figure at age 10 years 8 months still showing a great deal of anxiety and unsureness, and his human figure at age 11 years 11 months which is much better integrated but shows his great preoccupation with his developing sexuality. At this particular time, John shows more fears and concerns, yet also more awareness of other people and their feelings. This often occurs at the time of rapid prepubertal development.

John's parents have come a long way and still have a long difficult road to go in accepting and dealing with a severely disturbed child and planning for the future, unknown as it is, in a culture that accepts atypical behavior with a great deal of reservation and suspicion. John's parents use outside support well and understand that this is needed and try to give John their patience in the face of occasional despair, and a good deal of hope.

Mary: Mary, age five, appeared in her kindergarten smiling, sweet looking, and playing with minute dolls and horse figurines. She spoke in a sweet little voice, not to people, but addressed her figurines with endearments. Mary was not "there," and while her behavior seemed not grossly inappropriate for a first day of kindergarten, it did not change in any interactive manner and within a few days it became clear that she was not responding to any input of her new environment. We found later that changing or "learning" represented great danger to Mary and that she had to struggle to keep change away.

Her educational therapist gained her attention as Mary permitted her to enter her game with her figurines for short periods. The educational therapist did so by building very small "lessons" around the reality contexts of the horses, dolls, and their interaction. Their shapes, colors, and kinds, the activities represented, and most of all, the interaction between Mary and her educational therapist became the curricular focus. Entering the "real" world of her fantasy playmates provided the bridge for learning while sharing the perceptual and cognitive aspects of her safety world opened the sphere of wider learning.

Mary had personal reasons to need her special world; the educational therapist could acknowledge this and her awareness of Mary's need for her special space, allowing her to pace herself slowly enough so that Mary could risk peering into another learning world with her.

It took two years to help Mary into the world of the school-age child as a full participant; her own fears and tenuous hold on reality could recede as she found that knowing more about the real world and manipulating it with symbols, understanding, and using time modules, and experiencing cause and effect, made resorting to her fantasy gradually less necessary.

Mary is now able to learn at a rate appropriate to her age, though she is behind her age mates, and lives with other children in some give and take of work and play. She can say "no" and can establish herself as an individual.

Not only did the educational approach let Mary join her peers, but cognition itself provided her with the tools needed to cope in her life space. Her ability to have a reciprocal relationship with her therapist and to relate to other children in increasingly more appro-

6 years 6 months

MARY

9 years 5 months

I made myself too tiny.   —Mary
9 years 6 months

priate ways strengthens her ego functions sufficiently that she is able to hold on to that reality which is shared and to abandon her private world increasingly often. Her rocking has decreased and her face that used to recall an aged infant looks like that of a little girl. She is now making a transition into a regular class successfully.

About three years have elapsed since Mary's picture of herself as it appears on the cover and her picture of a girl drawn at age 9 years 5 months. Within three years Mary's human drawings progressed from an incomplete, hazy, sad, almost tragic figure to a coherent picture of a girl. The first picture lacks a body; the picture drawn at 9 years 5 months shows the head tilted sadly to its side; the picture of two figures, drawn at 9 years 6 months, shows a complete body and a certain assertiveness as well as the narcissism that Mary exhibits. When Mary drew the first of these pictures she commented, "I made myself too tiny." Later she drew the version making herself larger with visible facial features in contrast to the incomplete, unclear figure she drew at age 6 years 6 months.

Rodney: Rodney came to us from a therapeutic nursery school with a tentative diagnosis of retardation. He had been extensively evaluated by a number of clinics and the curious difficulty in relating to him and in describing his behavior suggested the presence of a significantly dysfunctional state. Also his parents' anguish and confusion mirrored the difficulties engendered not by a simply retarded but by a dysfunctional child with multiple problems in relating and information processing. As with most parents of such children, the pain of having to live with such a child had made them angry, anxious, and troubled.

Rodney had some physical problems, too; a penetratingly whiny voice, and an intrusive intensity of his communication which tended to reinforce the negative behavior of his caretakers. It appeared to us that a setting where his manifest behavior would be modified so that his caretakers could again become able to respond to him in a more positive manner would be required. Unfortunately such a person was only available in a setting with many more profoundly affected children and naturally it was hard for his parents to accept this, even though they were assured that this would only be a temporary placement.

During this year Rodney learned to listen more to others and to inhibit his incessant stream of anxiously compulsive talk. While he was evaluated as mildly retarded at the end of that year when in a short encounter with a psychologist he "tested" at that level, we insisted that he be managed not as a retardate but as a dysfunctional child whose real potential could not be appropriately assessed at this time.

Rodney has been in his special class for preacademic dysfunctional pupils the past three semesters. He reads well and can understand what he reads even if his special phobias, such as weather, are discussed. More important, Rodney now plays with his peers; he can take turns, he can express his feelings and accept the feelings of others. He can modulate his actions depending on how other people around him feel, he can look people in the eye, can be tender, or firm, and can be listening or talking in an appropriate manner.

Suddenly his art has become expressive and varied, having been obsessively stereotyped before. Rodney is becoming integrated in a regular class and can handle this experience increasingly better. His pictures and figures show this change in perceptiveness and responsiveness and reveal the high degree of intellect that is now becoming available for his use.

9 years

9 years 4 months

RODNEY

9 years 1 month

147

Pictures shown of Rodney indicate the change in his self-perception at the time that he also started to cope with his aggressive peers by drawing his cloud and weather pictures. While these two human drawings are only four months apart, age 9 years to age 9 years 4 months, there is a refinement and improvement in body image and a change to greater reality testing. Since that time Rodney has drawn cloud pictures almost every day, after which he can better deal with some of his feelings and with the tasks at hand.

RODNEY   10 years

This is a sunrise, and it's coming up, then it will be a sunny day, and Thanksgiving.

The clouds are cirrus, the fluffy clouds are cumulus.

That's my house.   —Rodney

As he draws these pictures his pervasive fears about clouds and weather seem to come under some cognitive control. These fears were further defused by involving him in study of weather science. The charting of his inner meteorology by charting the weather without seems to assuage his terror. At the same time, as his drivenness subsides he becomes more responsive to peers and is even beginning to show a sense of humor.

Jane: Jane was the youngest of seven children in a tumultous marriage which ended in divorce when Jane was nine years old. Jane smiling, sociable, seemingly comfortable was totally resistant to learning. All her teachers and even the psychologist who observed her briefly were convinced that she was significantly mentally retarded and she even managed to test in the retarded range at times while at others she would let out some of her native ability. Jane had learned to be the nonproducing, receiving baby. She was totally out of touch with anger and rage and her need to control, which she could so easily do by

JANE   7 years 2 months

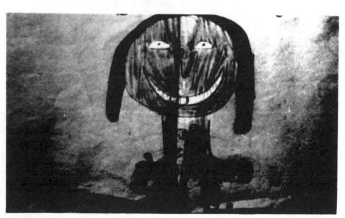

pretending to be an infant. Her picture at age 7 years 2 months shows the frozen angry state in which we found her. Her picture at age 10 years 6 months shows her eager and open to experience. Congruent management of both the affective and conative domain changed Jane's inner world as her art production shows.

JANE 10 years 6 months

Clark: In this group of dysfunctional children we have Clark who had no words two years ago and who now can speak in sentences, can be a group member in his class circle where for a time he had only sat there, alone within the crowd if made to do so, but in a far corner if permitted to be. He contacts the gaze of other children and his teachers, he shows pleasure and displeasure and is beginning to respond directly to other people.

Christine: Then there is Christine, who sweetly clung to any adult who would let her cling, staunchly avoiding any transaction other than being held or holding. Instead she now holds her real place in her group, owns her wishes and feelings, and engages people in some meaningful dialogue about information in the real world.

Jonathan: Jonathan, who spent six years in one of our special classes as a profoundly withdrawn, nonlearning boy, at age sixteen began to share feelings and aspirations with his teacher. He is attending regular classes with success and the years of academic and curricular therapy appear to emerge as useful bases for his educational coping. As one who seemed profoundly alone before, he suddenly counsels new members of the program, giving them hope. One day, as if out of the blue, he said to his teacher, *"I used to be a very sick child."*

Educational therapy with such profoundly handicapped students is slow work indeed, requiring one-to-one daily training sessions. As with all real cures, it is not a cure-all. What then justifies the expenditure of such energy, time, and money?

Successful habilitation of these children spells the difference between function and nonfunction, institutional living or community membership. The stakes are such that permission not to try does not exist. In terms of community funds, the dollar cost of even such daily attention over a number of years is infinitely smaller than lifelong institutional costs; however, the real cost in human potential that may be missed cannot be assigned any value.

The series of self-representation pictures show the increased integration of a body image and of the face as expressing increasingly more human features. This development occurs in normal growth, and may have occurred in these children without intervention; however, the usual career of such children suggests that developmental arrest is frequent. These children, as they acquired language and a time sense, referred to specific previous experiences with their relationship therapists in a way that suggests that such inputs did indeed help the development of structure in their perceptions, their self and body image, and their capacity to cope with information in a manner that made their behavior more goal-directed and socialized. At the same time, their sense of panic and confusion seemed to diminish as their coping improved.

When educational therapy cures the being-without-others, in a giant vacuum of time and space, devoid of expression, overcome by massive incoherent stimuli, and when it helps order the world to make it child size, the "cure" of educational therapy provides the very gift of life.

Chapter 6
CONCLUSION AND POSITION STATEMENT

I conclude that all is well," says Oedipus, and that remark is sacred. It echoes in the wild and limited universe of man. It teaches that all is not, has not been, exhausted. It drives out of this world a god who had come into it with dissatisfaction and a preference for futile sufferings. It makes of fate a human matter which must be settled among men.

—Albert Camus, The Myth of Sisyphus

The foregoing framework represents the distilled brew of practice with a "head" of theory concerning both administrative and care-giving activities. This presentation is made in the hope that many different care-givers will share their data on strategies and outcomes, too, so that a coherent body of experiential knowledge will soon be developed. Our sense of commitment and urgency is contained in the following position statement:

POSITION STATEMENT REGARDING SERVICES FOR SEVERELY DYSFUNCTIONAL CHILDREN

I. Delivery System Factors
    Schools are available community resources.
    Schools possess time-continuity factors.
    Schools already have child-focused personnel, many of whom are retrainable.
    Schools have an ongoing tax base, albeit a poor one, but better than none.
    Schools are ubiquitous.
    Schools provide "normal" role models at all levels.

II. Task Factors
    Need for support services to decrease entropy, hopelessness, helplessness, and withdrawal.
    Need for educational therapy inputs as primary conceptual and perceptual organizer.
    Need for ongoing administrative case coordination to ensure continuity, necessary services at auspicious times, assure parsimonious though effective deployment of professional time.
    Need for involvement of all significant others through strategies where their needs are utilized and met.

III. Philosophical Factors

If we profess concern for all children we express concern for the severely dysfunctional.

If we mean what we say, not just some available grant money but ongoing tax money must be supporting such pupils.

If the community mental health movement means to keep down the disordered functioning in each community, the disordered child must be helped to function in his school and his home.

Appendix

Annual Cost of School-Based Management of
Dysfunctional Children (1971-72)

Annotated Bibliography of Selected Sources

Commercial and Educational Films Valuable in
Child Development Training

Educational Materials

ANNUAL COST OF SCHOOL-BASED MANAGEMENT OF DYSFUNCTIONAL CHILDREN (1971-72)

Cost of educating 60 educationally handicapped students (about ten students severely dysfunctional, fifty more mildly affected) in five classes:

Teachers		$61,000
Administration, including Psychological Services		15,000
Educational Consultation		2,500
Mental Health Consultation		1,900
Secretarial		1,500
Paraprofessionals		2,000
Travel		150
Room allowances		1,500
Inservice		600
Capital Outlay		1,000
Per pupil instruction:	special	1,200
	regular	1,800
Maintenance		300
Total		$90,450
	Per pupil	$1,507.50

The severely dysfunctional students during their early years receive individual daily instruction for up to two years, at a cost of $1,350 per year. Three of the severely affected students received individual psychotherapy for from three to six months on a once per week basis, and with a specific treatment focus costing up to $750 per pupil. Thus we assume an additional expense of $1,500 plus mental health consultation time of about $180 per pupil for the severely dysfunctional pupils. For up to two years the cost for a severely dysfunctional (for instance, a mute autistic child) may be as high as $3,500. Compared to the cost of treatment center placement or even long-term, possibly lifelong institutionalization, this is a small price to pay, as treatment center fees now begin at $12,000 per annum.

ANNOTATED BIBLIOGRAPHY OF SELECTED SOURCES

Readings, films, and educational materials beyond the standard items are presented. These have been found useful by our staffs and participants in the U.C. Davis Extension, Davis Educational Therapy Summer Institutes.

Preservice Readings

Aries, Philippe. *Centuries of childhood.* New York: Random House, 1962.
    A history of family life.

Dennison, George. *The lives of children.* New York: Random House, 1969.
    Excellent description of the relationships of adults and children and children and children, presenting a highly creative approach to education.

Frost, J., and Hawkes, G. *The disadvantaged child: Issues and innovations.* Boston: Houghton Co., 1970.
    An outstanding anthology on children's problems.

Goffman, Irving. *The presentation of self in everyday life.* New York: Doubleday Anchor Books, 1959.
 A description of everyday behavior in observational terms; furnishes an important method of dealing with observation.

Haimowitz, M. L., and Haimowitz, N. R. *Human development: Selected readings.* New York: Thomas Knight Crowell Co., 1960.
 An outstanding anthology in the field of child development.

Henry, Jules. *Pathways to madness.* New York: Random House, 1969.
 Description of family interaction in detail. A guide to better, more careful observation of behavior in everyday living. Highly recommended.

Huizinga, Johan. *Homo ludens: A study of the play element in culture.* Boston: Beacon Press, 1950.
 This is the outstanding background presentation to understand the function of play in learning.

Jung, Carl G. *Man and his symbols.* New York: Doubleday, 1964.
 A superb introduction to man, his myths and his arts.

LaBarre, Weston. *The human animal.* Chicago: University of Chicago Press, 1954.
 A presentation of an articulated picture of the human being as an evolving, but very special biological entity.

Luria. A. The functional organization of the brain. *Scientific American,* March, 1970, **222**, 66-78.
 An exposition of the organization and interrelation of the brain; difficult to read but rewarding when understood.

Menninger, Carl. *The vital balance.* New York: Viking Press, 1963.
A discussion of "the life process in mental health and illness." Excellent descriptions of "mental health."

Mumford, Lewis. *The myth of the machine.* New York: Harcourt, Brace and World, Inc., 1966.
Excellent background on the problems of man, modern civilization, consciousness and creativity.

Murphy, L. R. *The widening world of childhood: Paths toward mastery.* New York: Basic Books, Inc., 1962.
Probably the best basis to understand the concept of coping and the development of coping mechanisms.

Inservice Readings

Bruner, Jerome. *On knowing.* Boston: Harvard University Press, 1962.
A most lucid exposition of the affective role in cognition and the role of the unconscious in the learning process.

Caplan, Gerald. *Concepts of mental health and consultation.* Washington, D.C.: Children's Bureau Publications, 1959.
A simple presentation of the newer concepts of consultation.

Hall, E. T. *The silent language.* New York: Doubleday, 1959.
Nonverbal communication.

Hall, Edward T. *The hidden dimension.* New York: Doubleday, 1966.
Space and time as language signal systems.

Hesse, Herman. *Demian.* New York: Bantam Books, 1925.
The growing up of the young male. Rules and roles.

Lewis, Howard R., and Streitfeld, Harold S. *Growth games.* New York: Bantam Books, 1970.
> Excellent source on awareness training, the expansion of perception and the use of fantasy.

Mead, Margaret, and Wolfenstein, Martha. (Eds.) *Childhood in contemporary cultures.* Chicago: Phoenix Books, 1955.
> A great help in learning to look at the behavior of children and families.

Phillips, John L. *The origins of the intellect: Piaget's theory.* San Francisco: W. H. Freeman & Co., 1969.
> A simplified exposition of Piaget's major theories.

Piaget, Jean. *Science of education and the psychology of the child.* New York: Orion Press, 1970.
> An outline of the basic tenets of Piaget's structural developmental approach.

Sarason, Seymour. *The culture of the school and the problem of change.* Boston: Allyn & Bacon, 1971.
> Excellent source on the school as an institution.

Schefflen, Albert E. *Body language and the social order.* Englewood Cliffs, N. J.: Prentice-Hall, 1972.
> Clear, readable introduction to the communication behavior involved in behavior control.

Sommer, Robert. *Personal space: The behavioral basis of design.* Englewood Cliffs, N. J.: Prentice-Hall, 1969.
> Space—its meaning and message.

Thomas, Alexander, Chess, Stella, and Birch, H. G. *Temperament and behavior disorders in children.* New York: New York University Press, 1968.
> Presentation and description of temperamental factors in children and parents.

Readings in Academic Therapy

Ashton-Warner, Sylvia. *Teacher.* New York: Simon & Schuster, 1963.
> The "organic" vocabulary.

Borton, Terry. *Reach, touch and teach.* New York: McGraw-Hill, 1970.
> An excellent discussion of affective ego-psychology education, viewing the learner's concern in developing curriculum.

Bush, Wilma Jo, and Giles, Marian Taylor. *Aids to psycholinguistic teaching.* Columbus, Ohio: Merrill, 1969.
> A language orientation for teaching practice.

Ekstein, R., and Motto, Jerome. *From learning to love to love of learning.* New York: Reiss Davis Child Center Publication, 1969.
> Ego psychology of education.

Hellmuth, Jerome. (Ed.) *Cognitive studies, Volumes I and II.* New York: Brunner Mazel Publishers, 1970 and 1971.
> An anthology of concept formation, normal and abnormal, structure and process.

Myklebust, Helmer R. *Progress in learning, Volumes I and II.* New York: Grune & Stratton, 1967 and 1971.
> An excellent survey of diagnostic and management problems in the learning disabilities utilizing a very inclusive and wide approach. A must for basic reading.

Smith, Robert M. *Teacher diagnosis of educational difficulties.*
Columbus, Ohio: Merrill, 1969.
   An excellent basis for the formulation of teaching objectives.

Weinstein, Gerald, and Frantini, Mario. *Toward humanistic educa-tion: A curriculum of affect.* New York: Praeger, 1970.
   An outstanding presentation of an ego-oriented curriculum.

The Ego-Dysfunctional Child and Behavior Management

Axline, Virginia. *Dibs.* New York: Ballantine Books, 1968.
   A *must* for child-serving staff.

Bettelheim, Bruno. *The empty fortress.* Glencoe, Illinois: The Free
Press, 1963.
   Excellent discussion of internal problems of disturbed children.

Bettelheim, Bruno. *Love is not enough.* Glencoe, Illinois: The Free
Press, 1955.
   Use of staff and insight strategies.

Donahue, George T., and Nichtern, Sol. *Teaching the troubled child.*
New York: Free Press, 1965.
   A basic introduction to the dysfunctional child.

Ekstein, Rudolf. *Children of time and space, of action and impulse.*
New York: Appleton-Century-Crofts, 1966.
   Description of severely disturbed children.

Erikson, Erik H. *Insight and responsibility.* New York: W. W. Norton
and Co., 1964.
   One of the outstanding treatments of identity formation.

Fagan, Joen, and Shepard, Irma Lee. *Gestalt therapy now.* Palo Alto: Fines Inc., 1970.
> Excellent chapters on awareness, awareness training, the use of art and the management of situational approaches.

Hewitt, Frank M. *The emotionally disturbed child in the classroom.* Boston: Allyn and Bacon, Inc., 1968.
> Excellent source book on educational and behavioral programming for children.

Kramer, Edith. *Art as therapy with children.* New York: Schocken Books, 1971.
> Lucid and helpful.

Long, N., Morse, W., and Newman, R. *Conflict in the classroom.* (2nd ed.) Belmont, Calif.: Wadsworth Publishing Co., 1970.
> Anthology of the learning disability and the education of emotionally disturbed children. A must.

Mahler, Margaret, and Furer, Manuel S. *On human symbiosis and the vicissitudes of individuation, Volume 1.* New York: International Universities Press, Inc., 1968.
> In spite of the cumbersome title, an outstanding description of the atypical child.

Redl, Fritz. *When you deal with children.* New York: Free Press, 1966.
> Sections on life space interviewing, discipline and understanding children's communication are outstanding.

Riese, Hertha. *Heal the hurt child.* Chicago: University of Chicago Press, 1962.
> One of the basic books on educational therapy describing the

major psycho-educational deficits and looking at learning disorders and educational therapy from the point of view of the development of the self.

Trieschman, Albert E., Whittaker, James K., and Brendtro, Larry K. *The other 23 hours.* Chicago: Albine Publishing Co., 1969.
An excellent book on milieu therapy programming.

Dependable Periodical Sources

Academic Therapy Quarterly
American Journal of Orthopsychiatry
Annual Review of Child Psychiatry and Child Development
Journal of Childhood Schizophrenia and Autism
Journal of Learning Disabilities

Belles Lettres

Readings that sharpen observation, deepen feeling, heighten empathy of the conditions of childhood, change, and growing up.

Axline, Virginia. *Dibs.*
Baruch, Dorothy. *One little boy.*
Bettleheim, Bruno. *Truants from life.*
Bradbury, Ray. The world the children made. *Saturday Evening Post Stories, 1950.*
Calisher, Hortense. Time, gentlemen. From *Tales for the mirror.*
Cather, Willa. Paul's case. From *Youth and the bright Medusa.*
Collier, John. Thus I refute Beelzy. From *Hauntings.*
Gordimer, Nadine. Charmed lives. From *Six feet of the country.*
Green, Hannah. *I never promised you a rose garden.*
Hamson, Knut. *Pan.*
Hesse, Hermann. *Demian.*

Hughes, Richard. *High wind in Jamaica.*

Lawrence, D. H. The rockinghorse winner. From *Best Short Stories.*

McCullers, Carson. *The heart is a lonely hunter.*

McCullers, Carson. *A member of the wedding.*

Riese, Hertha. *Heal the hurt child.*

Rilke, Rainer Maria. *The notebooks of Malte Laurids Brigge.*

Stafford, Jean. *Boston adventure.*

Saki. Sredni Vashtar. From *The best of Saki.*

Sykes, Gerald. (Ed.) *Alienation: An anthology.*

Undset, Sigrid. *Kristin Lavransdatter, Volume I.*

COMMERCIAL AND EDUCATIONAL FILMS VALUABLE IN CHILD DEVELOPMENT TRAINING

The child and the adolescent are enmeshed in perpetual change, involving them simultaneously in a state of being and a process of becoming. Film, communicating both the isochronous—within each frame—and the sequential—with each consecutive frame— can convey the child's ambiguous awareness of change within his fluid present.

The voyeurism of the camera is able to invoke the experiential openness of the receptive child or adolescent as well as the fearful, closed defense against perception, by the camera moving from the beheld to the beholder in varying rhythms and positions. The camera permits an engagement with the ongoing process of personal experience by its faculty to shift from the observer to the observed, from the self to the other, from subject to object, from a view of the world by the small to the tall, from closeness to distance, from the victim to the victor, the abandoned to the abandoner, the caring and the cared for.

At another level, the shift from simultaneous to sequential modes provides an experience of the multilevel processes occurring within the self at any given time. The coexistence of inner and outer sensations and moods, the multiple response patterns using language, symbol, fantasy, and innumerable changes and distortions can be suggested only by a medium like the film: picture and sound, reality and fantasy, time lapse and speedup, color and mood, combine to represent global experiential states.

In the area of content, the film can speak of the ambivalence of emotions, the ambiguity of meaning, and the relativity of reality. The dramatic line is able to convey conflicting roles and expectations, and coexisting incompatible needs and goals with a few strokes of picture and dialogue.

Film sets the stage for the viewer so that he may become receptive to the moods and feelings before him. Both the process and the content of the growing-up experience become again vividly available, tapping and even increasing the reservoirs of empathy, awareness, and concern that are needed in dealing helpfully with dysfunctional people.

Selected Films

A Member of the Wedding
> Portrays the inevitable confrontation with growing up—here in terms of a painful awareness of the need to abandon a "safe," known, tomboy role for the yet unknown role of the emerging woman. This film presents well the preconscious awareness of an impending developmental task in evoking behaviors and emotions which foretell change.

Rikshah Boy

A tender film showing the need for a male model for a young boy and the ambivalence created between him and his mother by his needed attachment.

The Little Fugitive

This film is photographed at the child's eye level. It is excellent in evoking changes in perceptual world by this change in visual angle. Good presentation of alternating states of bravado and fear in an anxious child.

The 400 Blows

An outstanding presentation of a mother-son love-hate relationship. Unmanageable anger and guilt lead boy to overt crime in a need to have his forbidden feelings punished and to find external limits. Excellent acting.

The Loneliness of the Long Distance Runner

Theme of mourning and anger, confusion of behavior in the presence of overwhelming instinctual pressures. This adolescent becomes unable to succeed in his need for self-punishment. There are outstanding subplots showing the social behavior of delinquent acting-out adolescent boys. Good casting of both youths and adults. A very rich film that does well with two showings to pick up different foci.

Phoebe

Story of a pregnant teenage girl. A beautiful portrayal of repeated inner rehearsal of intended communications, showing the moving forward and retreat in imagery and insight.

The Leather Boys
Sensitive description of shifting sexual identities of older adolescent boys, role experimentation, and role freezing. Also shows the use and involvement with fetish objects, such as the motorcycle.

The Red Balloon
A beautifully executed portrayal of the passive-receptive mode of childhood perception. Sets a feeling stage about perception and newness.

David and Lisa
Peer and adult relationships in mentally disordered, deprived adolescents. Somewhat case-history oriented.

Sundays and Cybele
A deserted young girl reinvests her emotional needs into an adult stranger. This film contains a vast emotional range in both child and adult; is beautifully photographed with rich symbolism and superb acting.

Scater Dater
A preadolescent boy experiences the sudden change from comfortably belonging to a peer group to being attracted to a girl. A brief, joyous, overtly conflict-free presentation creating some strong inner awareness of conflict and change.

Recommended Mental Health Films

Angry Boy   33 minutes
Describes the genesis and handling of anger.

Boundary Lines   10 minutes
  About tolerance, intolerance and fear; good discussion lead-
  off.

Children Growing Up with Other People   25 minutes
  Excellent presentation of feelings of children in the socialization process.

Children Learning by Experience   40 minutes
  Well used as a general lead-off to lay or professional child
  development series.

Children Who Love   28 minutes
  Cross-cultural focus; well used where audience is caught in
  ethnocentric focus.

The High Wall   30 minutes
  Origins and meaning of prejudice. Can be used to introduce
  formation of values, character development, aspects of anger
  and violence in delinquency.

James Was a Very Small Snail   60 minutes
  Good film on autism in childhood.

Mr. Finley's Feelings   10 minutes
  Excellent animated cartoon showing the conservation of feelings, introducing displacement, splitting off, somatization,
  and denial. Very "light" on the surface but involves audiences
  at strong feeling level.

Picture in Your Mind   16 minutes
  Outstanding artistically in message impace; depicts prejudice
  and how it defends the security of the lone individual. High
  impact movie.

Preface to a Life   30 minutes

    Role of expectations in outcome. Excellent discussion medi-
um for both lay and professional training groups.

Steps of Age   25 minutes

    Very evocative portrayal of aging; has a life-cycle framework
and, therefore, is useful in any developmental framework.

The Umbrella   28 minutes

    Good presentation of a case of childhood delinquency involv-
ing displaced anger at deprivation.

Out of Darkness   60 minutes

    Story of acute mental illness and recovery in an adolescent
girl.

Decision To Die   24 minutes

    On adolescent suicide.

Streetcorner Research   30 minutes

    In spite of title, film can be fruitfully used to show possibili-
ties of dialogue among disparate cultures—here streetcorner
delinquents and behavioral scientists.

EDUCATIONAL MATERIALS

Crates and boxes, especially man-size ones
Scrap lumber and tools
Pathway books
Pathway games
Twister
Languagemaster with teacher- and/or student-made materials
Bendable people (Creative Playthings)
Puppets, preferably made with and for the student
Sand, dirt, paint
Food to eat
Food to smell
Food to prepare
Places to dig in
Places to grow things
Places to be with people
Places to be alone
Large muscle exploration that lends play context; e.g., forts, multiple climbers, hoops, real fences to climb
     and most of all
A responsive human environment